ENTREPRENEURIAL MINDSET

A Guide on how to be a Successful Entrepreneur who is a Father and also a Husband

Table of Contents

INTRODUCTION

Entrepreneurs help bolster economic development, create jobs, and invent products or services that can make the world a better place. Being a successful entrepreneur requires outside-the-box thinking and larger-than-life ideas. Anyone can come up with a new idea, but building a successful business around it is an entrepreneurial challenge. The entrepreneurial mindset is unique in that one must be creative, communicative, and highly motivated to succeed, yet open to risk and failure.

It's not a big idea alone that paves the path to ultimate entrepreneurial success. Oftentimes the success or failure of a business comes down to the characteristics of the entrepreneur. It takes a unique aggregate of characteristics to meld one big idea into a fully-functional thriving business. Is there a certain amalgam of skills and traits which allows some entrepreneurs to become wildly successful?

Suffice it to say that there is no magical formula to succeed in business (if so, Harvard Business School would have patented it). However, there are certain characteristics that all aspiring entrepreneurs should cultivate to dramatically boost their odds for success. An entrepreneurial mindset, if you will, may mark the difference between a lucrative business and one which shatters the doors before the first year is over.

What Makes an Entrepreneur?

When an individual sets out to start their own business, they assume the majority of the risks and get most of the benefits. Entrepreneurship is a term used to describe the process of starting a business. Entrepreneurs are often viewed as innovators, inventors, and providers of new products, services, and/or business/or procedural concepts.

Anyone who has the ability to foresee market need and create new products or services is an entrepreneur. Profits, fame, and continuing development prospects are the rewards for successful entrepreneurship that takes on the risks of starting a new company. Losses and a decrease in market prominence arise from entrepreneurship that fails.

Here are some key takeways of who an entrepreneur is and what entrepreneurship consists of:

- A person who undertakes the risk of starting a new business venture is called an entrepreneur.
- An entrepreneur creates a firm to realize their idea, known as entrepreneurship, which aggregates capital and labor to produce goods or services for profit.
- Entrepreneurship is highly risky but also can be highly rewarding, as it serves to generate economic wealth, growth, and innovation.
- Ensuring funding is key for entrepreneurs: Financing resources include SBA loans and crowdfunding.
- The way entrepreneurs file and pay taxes will depend on how the business is set up in terms of structure.

How Entrepreneurship Works

In addition to land and natural resources, labor and capital, economists classify entrepreneurship as a resource essential to production. An entrepreneur combines the first three of these in order to produce or provide a product or service.

They typically create a business plan, hire employees, acquire resources and financing, and provide leadership and management for the company.

When starting a business, entrepreneurs are frequently confronted with a slew of challenges. The three most frequently cited as the most difficult are:

1. Overcoming bureaucracy
2. Hiring talent
3. Obtaining financing

The terms "entrepreneur" and "entrepreneurship" have never been defined by economists in a way that is clear and unambiguous (the word "entrepreneur" comes from the French verb entreprendre, meaning "to undertake"). Entrepreneurs were not included in classical and neoclassical economic models because they assumed that perfect information would be available to fully rational actors, leaving no room for risk taking or discovery. Entrepreneurship was not seriously considered by economists until the middle of the twentieth century.

Frank Knight and Israel Kirzner are two influential economists who pushed for the inclusion of entrepreneurs. According to Schumpeter, it is the entrepreneurs who create new products and services in the pursuit of profit. As the bearers of risk premiums in financial markets, Knight looked to entrepreneurs as the source of uncertainty. When it comes to entrepreneurship, Kirzner saw it as a process that eventually led to a breakthrough discovery.

CHAPTER ONE

THE HUMAN MIND OF AN ENTREPRENEUR

"Great minds think alike", but does this apply to entrepreneurial minds? Societies both past and present have enjoyed the benefits of innovations in technology, business, and information transmission. With all the advanced resources of society today, the world has seen a massive increase in global entrepreneurial activity, with many entrepreneurs becoming household names overnight. Bill Gates, Mark Zuckerberg, and Tom Ford.

"Well", you might think, "I'm certainly no Bill Gates." That's great, my friend because you don't have to be! At the GEC, the themes of inclusivity, the global entrepreneurial revolution, and the 'high-performance' ecosystems are aiming to broaden entrepreneurial thinking and open minds to the possibilities of economic growth that span across geographical, cultural, and social boundaries.

The mind of an entrepreneur is simply the human mind that is honed and adapted to persevere through challenges and take calculated risks when needed. There is no common mindset amongst business owners because each one of us has our unique talents. However, there are external factors that could hinder our creative mind and limit our ability to make the most of any entrepreneurial opportunities.

In our global ecosystem, governments and prevailing institutions can influence our strategy, our plan of action, and our vision. Haven't you ever wondered why the youth in the United Kingdom seem to be more prepared for employment, compared to the youth in Zimbabwe or Zambia? It is the institutional environment that shapes individual capabilities and perceptions.

Many private owners of businesses in African countries for example are not motivated to think globally, and therefore, the local businesses cannot compete with international organizations. This is further hindered by an intergenerational transmission of attitudes that dictate the mindset of young people, which is that hard work can only get you so far.

Therefore, the key differences amongst entrepreneurs lie in their culture and environment, which leads to a different mindset. This has been a recurrent and critical theme of the GEC 2019. Think about where you come from. Now think about the types of attitudes prevalent in your community, whether you come from a place where men and women are encouraged to take advantage of business opportunities, and whether your nation is taking an active role in the global ecosystem of entrepreneurship. The type of mindset you develop from a tender age can ultimately shape your perspective in business and, of course, life. If you are ambitious and driven, this is often interpreted as a zealous personality manifested from the mantra of Western ideology, "If you have a will, you will find a way."

Entrepreneurial minds cannot be given a specific blueprint and then used to identify other entrepreneurs. The key is to hone specific characteristics over time by engaging with your environment if you are fortunate enough to be given many opportunities.

Networking, strategizing, branding, and developing a competitive advantage will surely be aspects of the entrepreneurial lifestyle that you can embrace once you use the right resources. Exploring an entrepreneurial mind lies in exploring the potential. Are you someone who maintains an active role in your community, identifying needs that haven't been met, or have you got a value proposition for a product that you are trying to sell? If you are persistent, ambitious, goal-oriented, and creative, then you are well on your way to cementing an entrepreneurial mind.

Entrepreneure's Brains Are Wired Differently. Here's How to Use Yours Right.

If you're an entrepreneur or aspire to be one, you almost certainly have a "dopaminergic mind." This means you have a specific chemical tendency -- a genetic gift, really -- that does two things: It tends to make you more creative than other people, and it gives you an often-superior ability to channel your energies toward your goals. Here's how.

Dopamine, a chemical in your brain, is the "molecule of more": When you see something new, unusual, or potentially useful, you experience a pleasurable surge of interest. You feel it when you see a new coffee shop with a line out the door, find an email from a forgotten friend, or see someone cute across a crowded bar. Dopamine is released in your brain because you just discovered something new that will make your future better, richer, or more secure.

Some forms of "new" and "better" are obvious to everyone, like the new coffee shop or finding a great new book. Others aren't so obvious, like stumbling upon a novel solution to a stubborn problem. That's the basis of creativity: making new connections between things that were previously thought to be unrelated. These connections sometimes lead to new business opportunities. Sometimes they change the world. People with active dopamine systems, like entrepreneurs, are particularly good at recognizing these connections that everyone else misses.

Dopamine does something else, too: It gives you the ability to plan and calculate. In this way, dopamine provides us with a control circuit to complement that novelty-seeking circuit -- a complete neurochemical system to discover and then achieve what we want. It functions in every situation, whether earthshaking or mundane, driving us toward more. This biochemical process is no less than the engine of progress, which is the product of thinking up, creating, and providing new things. Therefore it makes sense that entrepreneurs would have more dopamine than other people.

And the more you understand how dopamine works, the better you can take advantage of it.

Don't Try to "fix" Yourself.

Dopamine is why entrepreneurs tend to be original thinkers and problem solvers. It is also the reason many entrepreneurs are absent-minded about the mundane details of the business. They live in a world of possibility rather than the ordinary world of the here-and-now. Take this story for instance.

Daniel is a psychiatrist. He once had a patient who was a successful entrepreneur -- and severely disorganized. His lack of interest in imposing order on the chaos of his life made doing business difficult. Like most entrepreneurs, when he identified a problem he set out to fix it. But, after speaking with Daniel, the two of them decided that the answer wasn't therapy or a pill. While that might have helped him diminish the disorder, it also would have diminished one of the things that made him a successful entrepreneur: his creative ideas for new businesses that bubbled up from his imagination. Still, the problem had a solution. Instead of changing the entrepreneur, they changed his situation. Daniel advised the man to hire an assistant. With order imposed by someone other than the entrepreneur, his problem was solved, his creativity and drive intact.

Permit Yourself to Wander.

One aspect of creative thinking is the association of things we wouldn't usually connect. The Beach Boys' Brian Wilson used ordinary objects as musical instruments. Steve Jobs worried about the aesthetics not of art but business machines. Countless startups have changed our lives by attaching technology to mundane elements of daily life. These radical improvements aren›t the product of rigid agendas and sterile conference rooms. They come from random collisions of unrelated things in the mind of the entrepreneur. But, for that to happen, the entrepreneur must allow their self to do something that looks like a waste of time -- doing what amounts to staring out the window.

The ability to make unusual connections comes from letting our attention wander through the abstract and the not-yet-existent. When you let your mind float, you are giving dopamine-free rein. Fortunately, that's easy to do. Go to a museum. Take a hot shower. Dance. Play an instrument. Whatever turns off your focus on the here and now, do it. It is in that unfocused mental space that dopamine remixes the multitude of memories, ideas, and abstractions in our imagination.

Recognize the Difference between Wanting and Enjoying.

Dopamine is the engine that drives the modern creation of wealth, but it also has a dark side: It makes us dissatisfied with the status quo. For many, this need to make things better is the driving force behind their entrepreneurship, but most discover that it's only half the path to a satisfying life. It is the experience in the here and now that provides the rest of human satisfaction, appreciating the things we've earned and the company of those we love. This isn't just a motto from a motivational poster. It has a biochemical foundation.

We are all familiar with the high-powered executive who can afford a beautiful beach house but who is too busy to sit in the sand. Dopamine powers such success, but other neurotransmitters in our brain are dedicated to something else entirely, the ability to appreciate the here and now -- to "stop and smell the roses," as the saying goes, or, simply, to enjoy things.

With their highly dopaminergic minds, entrepreneurs are naturally more attracted to pursuit than here-and-now enjoyment, yet they will find a new kind of pleasure when they explore this palette of feelings -- but it won't come naturally. They must choose to do so.

And as an entrepreneur, you can. We are not slaves to dopamine. While it inclines us toward wanting, the rest of life is enjoyed and comes with other unique pleasures.

A mindful appreciation of all the successful person has achieved is a true delight, and for many entrepreneurs, a fresh one. The power of dopamine balanced with the here-and-now chemicals of the senses -- wanting versus enjoying -- comprises the two halves of a satisfying life. In this way, we better appreciate why entrepreneurs do what they do, and expand further on what creative, enterprising men and women can achieve.

CHAPTER TWO

THE MENTAL HEALTH OF AN ENTREPRENEUR

Mental health is an integral and essential component of health. "Health is a state of complete physical, mental and social well-being and not merely the absence of disease or infirmity.» An important implication of this definition is that mental health is more than just the absence of mental disorders or disabilities.

What is Mental Health?

Mental health is a state of well-being in which an individual realizes his or her abilities, can cope with the normal stresses of life, can work productively, and is able to contribute to his or her community.

Mental health is fundamental to our collective and individual ability as humans to think, emote, interact with each other, earn a living, and enjoy life. On this basis, the promotion, protection, and restoration of mental health can be regarded as a vital concern of individuals, communities, and societies throughout the world.

Over the course of your life, if you experience mental health problems, your thinking, mood, and behavior could be affected. Many factors contribute to mental health problems, including:

- Biological factors, such as genes or brain chemistry
- Life experiences, such as trauma or abuse
- Family history of mental health problems

Mental health problems are common but help is available. People with mental health problems can get better and many recover completely.

Early Warning Signs

Not sure if you or someone you know is living with mental health problems? Experiencing one or more of the following feelings or behaviors can be an early warning sign of a problem:

- Eating or sleeping too much or too little
- Pulling away from people and usual activities
- Having low or no energy
- Feeling numb or like nothing matters
- Having unexplained aches and pains
- Feeling helpless or hopeless
- Smoking, drinking or using drugs more than usual
- Feeling unusually confused, forgetful, on edge, angry, upset, worried, or scared
- Yelling or fighting with family and friends
- Experiencing severe mood swings that cause problems in relationships
- Having persistent thoughts and memories you can't get out of your head
- Hearing voices or believing things that are not true
- Thinking of harming yourself or others
- Inability to perform daily tasks like taking care of your kids or getting to work or school

Mental Health of a Man as a Father

Like most men, I find myself unable to keep all the plates spinning nicely on their poles.

As a husband, father, and a working professional, the only time I can get anything done for me is while everyone is asleep. This is why I snuck downstairs at 5:00 am to work on this very important topic: dads need help.

More specifically, dads need help with their mental health.

The Modern Dad

The modern dad does way more today than the dads of our ancestors. Dads are pushing the boundaries of "manly" stereotypes and doing activities that our great-grandfathers would probably chuckle at. A few examples:

- Laundry
- Vacuuming
- Cleaning the house
- Diaper changes
- Cooking
- Shopping
- Arranging play dates

This is the abbreviated version of a very long list. Add occupational responsibilities and house/car maintenance, and it's no surprise that dads today are struggling to keep up with life's demands. I can hear the not-so-silent cries of the partners of these men shouting, "Welcome to my world!"

It's a valid point that I don't want myself or any man to forget. Mothers have long played the dual role of homemaker and full-time employee. Many work full-time, come home and clean, care for the kids, rinse and repeat. For whatever reason, many dads don't have the same knack for juggling all of those responsibilities. It is because of this that many are feeling the weight start to burden our mental health.

How Paternal Mental Health Affects the Family

Dads' emotional well-being is on the decline and, quite frankly, it is being overlooked. Recent research has demonstrated that when fathers' mental health declines, so does the quality of their co-parenting relationships. Families with fathers who struggle with mental health issues, particularly during early childhood, tend to have children with more difficulties managing their emotions and behaviors.

In other words: Fathers affect the quality and stability of the family.

It seems so intuitive, yet, psychological research largely undervalues and/or fails to acknowledge or incorporate dads. This spans the entire spectrum of fatherhood — from the perinatal period throughout all of the major milestones of being a dad — fathers are largely absent from psychological research.

What Are The Barriers To Care?

It is essential for fathers to seek care when they need it, however, so many don't. A few likely explanations include:

Men are left to figure things out when it comes to the transition to fatherhood. We are in the Dark Ages when it comes to supporting new fathers. Paternal mental health is a newer field of study, and a lot of the data is suggesting that the transition impacts fathers' mental health just as much as mothers.

Men are poorer treatment-seekers. This relates to the deeply ingrained cultural ideas about masculinity and how we as men are "supposed" to feel and behave. At a young age, boys and teens are told to "walk it off" and "man up." They are taught, sometimes explicitly sometimes not, that showing emotions is a sign of weakness. Thus, they grow up into men, and subsequently fathers, who struggle with acknowledging, communicating, and managing their emotions.

Men's options are a little more limited in mental health clinicians. Clinicians are not often equipped to navigate the complexities of working with men and boys, and there are several gender-specific issues that men and boys need attending to. The mental health landscape is primarily made up of clinicians who have been trained almost solely with female clientele (men don't seek treatment at the same rate that women do). Men don't have as many options — and the options they do have may not be best suited to their needs.

With these barriers in mind, it is essential for us to acknowledge paternal mental health and to encourage dads, and all men, to seek mental health care when they are struggling.

So, before I go back to the world of laundry and play dates, let me leave my fellow fathers with this:

You have the power to influence great change in your family and even the future generations that come after you. The decisions you make today, positive or negative, are being evaluated by your children. Set the example: when you need help, ask for it; feelings are real, don't ignore them; and, you are no less a man for doing so.

Dad's Mental Health can Affect the Entire Family

Becoming a parent is a huge developmental milestone, for moms and dads alike. A lot of changes happen immediately and although health professionals educate many new parents about what these changes look like for moms, very few hear about a man's transition into fatherhood.

Psychologically, men face some of the toughest developmental challenges when they become a father. They may also face challenges and changes in their relationship with their partner. As soon as a new baby enters the world, the need to listen, think critically and make difficult parenting decisions take center stage. At the same time, intimate relations with your partner are not a priority. Health experts believe many men who relied on their partners for emotional support and intimacy can be left feeling guilty, resentful, and confused as they try to figure out how to support their partners while sacrificing their support and need for intimacy.

Paternal Postpartum Depression

Fathers often face a new level of stress relating to their work performance and income. Recent studies show one in ten fathers get postpartum depression and nearly 20 percent are diagnosed with an anxiety disorder when a new baby arrives. Some studies say that up to 50 percent of new dads experience PPD if their partner is experiencing depression, too.

Society views men as stoic, self-sacrificing, and most importantly, strong. When men feel none of those things as new fathers, they don't want to admit it or seek help. Experts in paternal mental health say fathers are struggling and suffering from mental health difficulties at about the same rate as mothers. The majority of these mental health difficulties go unnoticed, undiagnosed, and untreated.

With the right knowledge and training, daughters, sons, mothers and other loved ones can be the difference for a father living with mental health difficulties. Knowing how to notice the signs of depression and other common mental health challenges can help more dads get the support they may need.

Watch for the Signs

Every person is different but there are several common depression symptoms. They include;

- o   Engaging in high-risk activities
- o   A need for alcohol or drugs
- o   Withdrawing from family and friends or becoming isolated
- o   Anger, irritability, or aggressiveness

- Feeling anxious, restless
- Loss of interest in work, family, or once-pleasurable activities
- Problems with sexual desire and performance
- Feeling sad, "empty," flat, or hopeless
- Not being able to concentrate or remember details
- Feeling very tired, not being able to sleep, or sleeping too much
- Overeating or not wanting to eat at all
- Thoughts of suicide or suicide attempts
- Physical aches or pains, headaches, cramps, or digestive problem

It's OK to Reach Out

Look for support from people who make you feel safe and cared for. The person you talk to doesn't have to be able to treat you; they just need to be a good listener.

Make face-time a priority. Phone calls, social media, and texts are great ways to stay in touch but they don't replace good, old-fashioned in-person quality time. The simple act of talking to someone face to face about how you feel can play a big role in easing symptoms of depression and keeping it away.

Try to keep up with social activities even if you don't feel like it. Often when you're depressed, it feels more comfortable to retreat into a shell, but studies show being around other people will make you feel less depressed.

Join a support group for depression. Being with others dealing with depression can go a long way in reducing your sense of isolation. You can also encourage each other, give and receive advice on how to cope, and share your experiences.

Entrepreneurs Mental Health

Being an entrepreneur is not easy. More than 9 out of 10 businesses fail, with up to 50% failing by year three. As the stats show, entrepreneurship – even for eventually successful founders – is more often about failure than success. The stress that this brings can affect significantly an entrepreneur's self-belief and can have an impact on an entrepreneur's mental health.

Research shows that one in four adults experience mental illness. Being an entrepreneur increases your risk further. Entrepreneurs are

50% more likely to report having a mental health condition, with certain conditions being more prevalent amongst founders and character traits that make them more susceptible to mood swings.

Entrepreneurs are:

- Twice as likely to suffer from depression,
- Six times more likely to suffer from ADHD,
- Three times more likely to suffer from substance abuse,
- Ten times more likely to suffer from bipolar disorder,
- Twice more likely to have suicidal thoughts.

"People who are on the energetic, motivated, and creative side are both more likely to be entrepreneurial and more likely to have strong emotional states. Those states can include depression, despair, hopelessness, worthlessness, loss of motivation, and suicidal thinking.

How Entrepreneurs Can Protect Their Mental Health

Entrepreneurship tends to be thought of as a glitzy way of life. A lot of that can be attributed to what's posted and seen on social media from the most successful entrepreneurs who show off their "freedom" and upscale lifestyle.

What people fail to understand is that this kind of life makes up a very small minority of entrepreneurs, and almost all of them didn't get to that point of success without years of struggle and financial hardship while building their companies.

In addition, what's shown on social media also isn't always a depiction of a person's real lifestyle.

Being an entrepreneur isn't about waking up on a remote island and sending out a few emails before hopping on a private jet to Italy. The business is a daily grind, even for those who have successfully built their company into a money-making revenue machine.

It's not easy deciding to start and build a business, reflected in a study where 72% of entrepreneurs self-reported mental health concerns. The study also noted that entrepreneurs were significantly more likely to report a lifetime history of depression, ADHD, substance use, and bipolar diagnosis.

A newly formed small business can't grow or make money in the early stages if its leader doesn't have the "hustle" mentality to grind day in and day out.

Here are a few ways that entrepreneurs can protect their mental health throughout the stressful, but rewarding journey of creating and building their own business.

1. Take care of your finances

Like in any area of life, financial issues are the number one reported cause for stress and anxiety among entrepreneurs. Some people put their entire life savings into the startup with nothing to fall back on.

Research shows that 39% of small business owners use cash to fund their companies. While that's a method that has worked for a few, it's not recommended and could leave someone in a tough spot if the company doesn't work out.

The start-up journey is stressful enough, to begin with, and putting everything into a basket that fails 90% of the time is not smart. It's important to make sure there's a financial cushion to live on for at least three to six months.

If that's not possible, consider working a part-time job that allows for flexible hours. Another idea is having a side hustle that brings income like having a rental company or curating an investment portfolio.

The biggest takeaway is to try and leave as much money on the table to take care of the personal side of things and find a way to still bring in an additional income stream at the same time.

2. Don't be afraid to delegate

Another quick way to overheat and face an even higher level of stress is trying to do everything by yourself. Even if the startup isn't in a place to take on full-time employees quite yet, there are endless resources available to help a business outsource certain tasks.

This is important because burnout can happen very quickly when a business is forming, and that process tends to speed itself up if the founder is trying to do everything on their own.

Another option to avoid wearing down is going into business with a partner. Typically, each person would be an expert in a certain area of the company which would not only take things off one's plate but also is beneficial in driving the business forward.

3. Surround yourself with the right people

When beginning the entrepreneur journey, it's important for a person's mental well-being that they are surrounded by positive influences.

There will be some friends and family members that question the decision to leave corporate life with a steady paycheck behind. Remember, they come from a position of care and love, but they aren't entrepreneurs.

Surround yourself with mentors who have been successful as an entrepreneur. Ask them for advice and guidance through the beginning of the start-up journey and continue to develop that relationship and expand a professional network as the business grows.

Mental health can easily deteriorate with the wrong people giving the wrong advice or pushing one's self to the point of burning out. Checking in with one's emotions will help to ensure that self-care stays a top priority.

CHAPTER THREE

SELF-AWARENESS FOR ENTREPRENEURS

What is self-awareness? Why is it important for entrepreneurs? What if I think I am already self-aware? How can I become more self-aware?

What does it take to be a successful entrepreneur?

Ask most people and they'll probably head straight for creativity, drive, or resilience.

I want to talk about self-awareness. Specifically, why self-awareness is so important for entrepreneurs and how we can become more self-aware.

What is Self-Awareness?

Self-awareness can be defined as the conscious knowledge of one's character, motivations, strengths, and weaknesses.

This needs adding to; self-awareness is also about knowing how you are perceived by others and how your actions affect them.

As an entrepreneur, it is also about how this affects your business.

Why is Self-Awareness Important For Entrepreneurs?

1. Is entrepreneurship right for you?

This is a reality check question for anyone thinking about starting their own business. The process can be challenging; long hours, personal sacrifice, financial difficulties, tough decisions, and, of course, failure.

Aspiring entrepreneurs need to be self-aware enough to honestly ask whether they possess the skills and resilience necessary to survive and succeed.

2. What really drives you?

Being self-aware enough to find out what motivates and drives you is a critical step in any entrepreneurial journey.

What is your vision?

What problem are you passionate about solving?

What legacy do you want to leave behind?

If you cannot honestly answer these questions, you may struggle. How can you ensure that you remain goal-focused unless you truly know what you want? How can you inspire others without having a clear purpose and vision?

If, on the other hand, you are self-aware enough to know what really drives you, remaining focused, authentic, and inspiring will come more easily.

3. Leverage Your Strengths

As an entrepreneur, you will probably need to play the role of 'all-rounder' and wear more than one hat on most days. Even so, your time is precious and limited (I keep asking Santa for a 36 hr day but, year after year, he's failed to deliver), which means that you need to know where you can have the greatest impact.

For this reason, you must identify what your strengths are and leverage them as best as you can.

4. Address your weaknesses

Being self-aware enough to identify your weaknesses is critical. Entrepreneurs need to be able to adapt and improve quickly but to do so, they need to know exactly what needs to be improved.

In this respect, self-awareness provides entrepreneurs with an opportunity (and a necessary starting point) for self-improvement.

As your business grows, you will find yourself needing to hire staff. As you do, being self-aware will ensure that you can hire staff who are strong where you are weak.

In the process, self-awareness will enable you to simultaneously fill any 'skills gaps' in your business and build a team with complementary but not overlapping strengths.

5. Building team and culture

It is often said that 'team is everything' when growing a business. It is not enough for your team to be individually talented; they also need to work together collaboratively and effectively. The right team culture has to be in place, along with sufficient levels of mutual trust and respect.

As an entrepreneur, your staff will look to you as an example of how to act.

What is your work ethic?

Are you open-minded to the views of others?

Do you remain helpful when stressed?

Do you accept responsibility for your mistakes?

How, in other words, do you treat others?

Remaining self-aware and tuned into the way you treat other people is essential to creating both the right culture and an effective working environment.

6. Selling

When you run your own business, you are going to have to sell. This could involve selling your product or service to clients, but it could also involve selling your vision to staff or selling your financial credibility and future (meteoric) growth to investors.

How do you come across during the sales process? Pushy and overbearing? Uncertain and lacking confidence? Arrogant and presumptuous?

Self-awareness can provide an insight into how you come across to other people, something that is especially useful in a sales context where establishing rapport and rapidly building trust is critical.

7. Work-life balance

As mentioned above, being an entrepreneur can bring with it a very particular set of challenges in the form of long hours, stress, strained cash flow, and the need to place the business before anything else in your life.

Despite this, and as the most valuable asset in your business, you need to ensure that you remain as healthy, fit, happy, and mentally stable (yes, mentally stable!) as possible.

Due to the relentless stresses and demands of entrepreneurship, this is often easier said than done. It can often feel impossible to not travel at 100mph — or realize you are doing so until you hit a brick wall!

Here, once again, self-awareness is vital. By listening to your body and mind, by recognizing when you are struggling, by realizing when you need sleep and, more generally, by prioritizing your health and wellbeing, you will (contrary to what it may feel like) be acting in the best interests of your business.

I'm Pretty Self-Aware Already, Thanks!

Are you reading this and thinking 'I'm already self-aware, thank you very much?

This point of view is not uncommon and many people, entrepreneurs included, assume that they are sufficiently self-aware and tuned into their motivations, strengths, and weaknesses.

The first thing to say is that irrespective of how self-aware you are, actively working on becoming more so is only ever a good thing.

Secondly (and here's the rub), people who lack self-awareness are unlikely to recognize that they need to be more self-aware.

All entrepreneurs should, therefore, invest time and effort into becoming more self-aware, regardless of whether they feel they are already self-aware enough.

Becoming More Self-Aware

1. Be more conscious

Try to be more conscious of the way you act, why you act a certain way and how others react to you, and the decisions you make.

2. Make time for self-reflection

Make self-reflection a daily habit. If this is not already part of your routine, don't expect it to just happen; rather, you will need to plan, make the time, remove distractions, and proactively reflect on your day and your actions.

3. Keep a record

As humans, we are prone to forget. We also tend to adjust our memories of the past based on the present. As such, keeping a journal/diary of key events, problems, successes, and decisions may prove incredibly useful.

4. Capture and revisit your goals

Having a clear understanding of your goals, fears, and motivations is an important part of self-awareness. Write these down, put them aside and review them at a later date (what do you think of the person who wrote them?).

5. Exercise objectivity and humility

This sits at the core of this whole issue. You need to be able to view yourself and your actions objectively, which requires you to stand back, assess yourself honestly, and accept that you're going to suck at times!

Keeping the Socratic paradox — "I know that I know nothing" — at the front of your mind will help here.

6. Seek feedback

Proactively and periodically ask for feedback from the people around you, both in the workplace and in your personal life.

7. Take a test

Taking a personality test can help introduce a structured and objective approach to understanding more about your personality.

There's a long list of tests out there but a few of the better ones are the Myers-Briggs assessment, the Predictive Index, the DISC assessment, the StrengthsFinder assessment, and the Entrepreneurial Aptitude Test.

And finally, whether you are self-reflecting, keeping a record, seeking feedback, or taking a test, ensure you are self-aware enough to accept whatever it says about you!

7 Ways Entrepreneurs Can Master Self-Awareness

The first steps toward true success are always inward. Successful entrepreneurs know how to master who they are and harness their inner power, instincts, and intuition.

Knowing themselves with clarity leads them to the right deals and business ventures. If they do not have acute self-awareness, they will come up against the counterforce of out-of-control emotions, leading to their downfall. With self-awareness, it's possible to better predict the power relationships necessary for success.

1. Being inwardly directed.

Successful leaders are inwardly motivated by a drive or force that propels and motivates them to work hard to master their skills. This inner force is not unique to the profoundly successful. Everyone has this capability and each person has something distinctive to offer since no one is a repeatable phenomenon in this universe.

This inner direction is what guides successful entrepreneurs toward attaining their goals because they are driven to express who they are through their work. Each individual has a personal legend to live and leave. Going inward is their first place to tap. This inner direction grants people the ability to know themselves well enough to master who they are and how they make decisions.

2. Learning the ropes.

In any novel situation in business, an entrepreneur must learn the ropes. Skilled leaders are not afraid to start at the beginning because the more they know the bottom-line mechanics of a business, the more successful their ventures will be over the long term.

The average person tends to enter new deals with a lot of excitement initially and then lose his or her drive after emotions such as boredom, impatience, fear, or confusion gain sway. Successful entrepreneurs master these emotions, follow the lead of others, learn the rules and observe how things fit together.

Through this process, they develop the confidence needed to master their destiny. They are humble and know that with practice comes fluency.

To be successful, take this same path and be humble to learn the ropes. This is how to move from a follower to a leader of a business.

3. Demonstrating emotional control.

Great leaders have mastery over the inner world of their emotions. They are sharp about knowing when to use their emotions to push for power and attainment and when to pull back and use self-control to get what they want.

Successful entrepreneurs do not let fear or anger take over and control their decision-making capabilities. Fear and anger make it difficult to reach mastery as these emotions disconnect people from rational thought. And rational thought keeps someone in touch with the whole battlefield, creating the space for good decision-making and propelling the leader beyond petty emotions toward success. Self-control is a necessary ingredient for driving success.

4. Taking risks.

Accomplished leaders understand that self-awareness brings a sense of certainty in tough decision-making situations. This self-awareness enables them to make quicker and more efficient assessments in tough moments.

Their self-knowledge clears space so they can cut through the confusion, making their commitment to decisions more fluid. Successful leaders use observation and learning to become experts at knowing patterns of business and behavior, enabling them to take more risk with less loss.

5. Showing patience.

Accomplished entrepreneurs have the maturity and experience to have patience. Sometimes closing certain deals requires a combination of strategy, realigning, striking out, losing, and going back to the drawing board to start again.

Patience helps leaders look beyond what's before them and wait as the chips fall into place without lashing out impulsively in a negative way and destroying the opportunity. Leading successfully sometimes means doing by not doing and seeing that it all gets done.

6. Cultivating wisdom.

Learning to master the inner world of reactions is what drives proficient leaders to make sound decisions, learn from their mistakes and not quit. Wisdom comes from being willing to lose little battles to win the war. There's no way to succeed without first having the ability to manage the inner world of reactions, fear, and complacency.

With wisdom comes persistence and proficient leaders recognize this as the key to success. When others give up, they keep going. Persistence generates success inwardly and outwardly in the world of observable results. Having this wisdom keeps leaders on the continual climb to the top.

7. Exhibiting curiosity.

Leaders are usually not satisfied with only a certain level of success. Once one level has been secured and mastered, an inner tug calls for checking out what's at the next level. This pull is driven by an emotional force of curiosity and desire.

It involves a curiosity to see how much more can be created and achieved. Curiosity stimulates personal growth. When the desire to succeed arises out of this curiosity, then success has no limits. A lack of curiosity leads to contentment with what is. Great leaders are never content.

All people can be masters of their destiny. The counterforce that each desiring entrepreneur has to master is his or her reactive inner world. Great results come from the matrix of managing when to push and when to back off.

This means having self-knowledge. Stay curious in terms of career. Curiosity inspires creativity and creativity is where all new ideas stem from. This is how leaders become mavericks. They pay no attention to fitting in. They know that their success often comes at the expense of not belonging. Belonging isn't their concern. Succeeding, expanding, and creating are their concerns.

Why You As An Entrepreneur Can't Do It All

As entrepreneurs, we think we are the only ones who can get the job done. We have a hard time letting go of the reins and letting other qualified people help us in areas where we need assistance. But if you don't learn to allow others to help you -- especially in your areas of weakness -- you set yourself up to become overwhelmed and frustrated.

I'm a creative person, and can sometimes be too creative. When I started my website for my business, nothing seemed to turn out the way I envisioned it or run the way it should. Why? I could not let go of the fact that I was not a web designer and couldn't do it all. Being a designer and a creative individual are two different things. I spent countless hours learning to build a website instead of hiring someone with the skill and working on other things that needed to get done.

I learned quickly that I needed employees with strengths where I didn't so that there would be balance in my business. Find your super strength and exploit it, while you let others take care of things that slow you down.

Delegating is supposed to make your life easier, not complicate it even more. When you implement a system or bring on new people to take over certain tasks, make sure it's efficient so that you are not creating even more tasks for yourself. The more you delegate tasks to others, the more time you will have to spend on paving the way for your company. However, delegating only works when done effectively.

Hire the right people for the right task, make sure they have an understanding of your business and mission.

Know everyone's strengths so that you delegate effectively.

Explain the tasks to employees, and don't assume they know exactly what to do on their own. Be specific on the work to be done.

In the beginning, you're not just the CEO of your business. You're the customer service rep, you're in charge of scheduling, planning, bookkeeping; the list goes on, but as your business grows, and you hire a team, they become partially responsible for the success of your business.

Learn When to Say No.

Saying the word "no" is hard to say for most young entrepreneurs. You feel like you need to do it all, multitask your way through everything, while never slowing down. Taking on everything may seem like a good idea because it gets your name out there and you make great contacts that would be perfect for your business. I thought the same thing at first, but quickly learned I took on way more than I could handle. I also hated saying "no" to people because I did not want to miss out on an opportunity. The truth is, saying no is better than promising something you're not going to be able to accomplish in the amount of time something needs to be done. Don't be afraid to say no to people, if you think it might take away from your business instead of growing your business.

As a young entrepreneur taking risks, you are going to make mistakes, but many times that is the best learning experience you can get. Don't be afraid to mess up.

CHAPTER FOUR

HOW TO ACHIEVE WORK-LIFE BALANCE AS AN ENTREPRENEUR

You wanted to become an entrepreneur to be your boss, make an unlimited amount of money, and most importantly, to have freedom of choice. Right?

Can you honestly say that freedom of choice is your current reality?

Face it. As an entrepreneur working to build a successful business, you have a lot of responsibilities.

A few include:

o   Servicing existing customers' needs
o   Securing new customers
o   Selling current products or services
o   Developing new products or services
o   Building strategic relationships

Well, you get it.

There is just so much that has to be done as an entrepreneur that there is little time to spare. Twenty-four hours in a day, minus the sleep, doesn't seem like that much time when you have a business to operate and build.

Every day as an entrepreneur seems like a marathon. You're exhausted after putting in long hours of work, but you wake up the next day and do it all over again.

Let's ask a serious question. With so many hours spent on your business, how is your personal life going?

- Your spouse or romantic partner probably constantly nags you about the lack of time you spend together.

- If you have kids, you probably don't spend as much time with them as you would like, which could do serious damage to your relationship with them in the future.
- Your friends don't even invite you out anywhere anymore because they know that your business is your life.
- You are not even aware of what is going on in the outside world—all you know is your business.

Is Pursuing Success as an Entrepreneur Worth Risking so Many Relationships and Losing Your Personal Life?

If your ultimate goal is simply to be wealthy, then you probably don't mind risking the loss of relationships and not having a personal life.

However, entrepreneurship is ultimately about enjoying the fruits of your labor, right?

You don't want to become a scrooge—someone who has financial wealth, but never experiences the interpersonal joys it can bring.

As your business becomes more busy and stressful, you have to look for ways to perfectly balance your business life and personal life.

What is Work-Life Balance?

Work-life balance is simply a healthy balance between your work life and your personal life.

Achieving such a balance doesn't necessarily mean that you need to put an equal amount of hours into both your work life and personal life.

Realistically, being an entrepreneur, your business is going to require a great deal of your time. You can't neglect this responsibility, especially in the beginning, if you want to be successful.

When you wake up, your business and the day's tasks are on your mind. Before you go to sleep, you think about what was accomplished during the day and how close you are to achieving your overall business goals.

You could view your business success as personal success, but that shouldn't be the case. Your business can provide you with wealth, but money can't replace real people and real experiences.

Although your loved ones will certainly enjoy the lifestyle provided by your success, they may also come to resent you because your time is never spent with them.

This is a commonplace experience that many people in business are aware of.

We all want to enjoy our family, have fun with our friends, and experience life, but sometimes it's a struggle to do all these things and still keep our businesses afloat.

On the other hand, we didn't become entrepreneurs only to struggle financially.

So as much as we want to achieve a work-life balance, we aren't willing to sacrifice our ability to achieve financial success to get there.

Does this make us selfish?

It's just a practical way of looking at things. After all, if you don't get the work done, then who will?

You know that a perfect balance between your work life and personal life can't be achieved, but you can take actions that make your daily life more manageable and which allow you to handle both parts of your life.

And you have no excuse for not achieving this balance. If billionaire entrepreneurs make it a requirement to schedule time for their personal lives while maintaining their busy schedules, so can you.

- **Richard Branson:** Branson says the keys to maintaining balance for him are flexibility, delegating work, and prioritizing time for fun. *"I find that technology is a great help—I use phone calendars, email reminders, and mobile reminders to maneuver my way to each meeting, event, and party. You can also use these things to make sure you have time to eat regularly and that you can get a good sleep. My family is the center of my life, so wherever I am in the world, when I have a few minutes, I talk to my wife and kids."*
- **Warren Buffet**: Buffet's decision to stay in Nebraska rather than move to New York City—where life is a constant rush and expen-

sive—has helped him maintain a more balanced life. *"You may need to do fifty things a day in New York, but I'd rather do some reading in my office and do one to two things a day and do them well."*

How to Achieve a Better Work-Life Balance

The first step to creating a work-life balance is prioritizing by importance the activities that will occur during the course of your day.

Implementing a balanced schedule will allow you to make sure you are including things that matter to you personally, beyond just sales calls and marketing messages.

Implementing Your Schedule

As an entrepreneur, operating within a strict schedule can be hard to achieve, because no two days are the same. When something within your business needs your attention, you may feel like you need to drop everything you are doing to address the problem.

While it may be necessary to attend to some issues straightaway, every little thing that occurs doesn't need your immediate attention.

Let's say it together:

- o Every email doesn't need your immediate response
- o Every text doesn't need your immediate response
- o Every phone call doesn't need your immediate response

If it isn't a specific activity that you have allocated time to in your schedule, then it is a distraction.

The best way to plan your daily activities is to create your schedule for each day the night before. This way you can hit the ground running in the morning.

When you plan things the night before, you remember what occurred earlier in the day—what you achieved and what you didn't get to. One of the easiest ways to do this is to keep notes of your activities throughout the day so that you can review why they were or weren't achieved, and plan accordingly.

But remember, we aren't focusing only on business activities. Work-life balance means that our personal life is given the proper attention it needs.

Your day can't consist of only business activities.

Even though working on your business will dominate your schedule, you will have to make the time and effort for your personal life.

Scheduling your Day

You're an entrepreneur so an early start to your day should already be something that you do. Many successful entrepreneurs are early morning risers. The earlier you get up the more you get done.

Provided below is an example of how your schedule could flow to achieve a work-life balance. The example used here is just a standard schedule — yours may be more complex.

5:00am – 6:30am

- Wake up
- 30 min for a light workout or meditation
- 30 min for breakfast
- 20 min to shower and dress

6:30am – 7:30am

- 5 min to go over the schedule from the night before
- 15 min to check and respond to emails
- 15 min to catch up on current news
- 20 min to read the book of the week/month

7:30am – 12pm

- Begin your work scheduled for the day
- The task with the most importance is given priority attention

  o You want to dedicate a lot of time to making progress on or completing this task, but don't drag it out. Tight time restraints force you to be more productive. Try to spend no more than two hours on this 'most important task.'

- As your first task is completed, move forward to the next

  o Dedicate no more than an hour to each. It may seem impossible to accomplish much within these tight time constraints, but you're forcing your brain to be sharply focused.

12pm – 1pm

- 30 min to eat lunch
- 30 min clear your head and get re-energized

  o Take a walk
  o Power nap
  o Read a book

1pm – 6pm

- Revisit your priority task if it has not been completed

  o No more than an hour and a half spent on finishing it up

- Manage your business processes

  o 1 hour to follow up with clients via phone or email
  o 30 min to engage on social media and other networks
  o 30 min to check your analytics and backend details

- Begin finishing up your day at the office

  o Go over the work you completed and note the tasks that will require further attention

6 pm – 9 pm

PERSONAL TIME!*

- Attend kid's game or recreational activity
- Eat dinner with spouse/family
- Spend quality time with friends

10pm – 11pm

- 30 min to review your day and set your schedule for the next day
- 30 min to read a book before going to sleep

You will notice that the majority of your day was spent working on your business, and only three hours were dedicated to your personal life. That might seem like a small amount of time, but being an entrepreneur is a time-consuming endeavor.

Achieving financial freedom requires sacrifices.

You don't want to simply set scheduled time in the personal category like every other appointment, because it makes people feel like they're just a part of your schedule rather than being an important part of your life. Make sure to make time for the people who matter to you, but also make sure you want to spend time with them—you aren't just "fitting them in."

Make Compromises

The perfect work-life balance isn't achievable, but that doesn't mean that you can't still try to make those in your personal life happy.

Let your loved ones know that they will have to be patient so that you can focus your time on building a successful business. You are working hard to improve their lives, so communicate this to them and set a timeline for the goal to be accomplished.

Let your family know that when you achieve a certain goal, they'll be rewarded for giving you the time to work. Maybe it's a family day outing or a family vacation. Giving your family something to look forward to may help them understand why you work so hard.

Communication is the key.

Just because you understand the importance of spending so much time working on your business, doesn't mean that those around you do. If your work schedule for the day may take more time than usual, let it be known and promise that you'll make the time up.

Keep people informed so that they know what to expect.

Develop Systems that Create Balance

The only way real work-life balance can occur is if you focus on working on your business, not working in your business.

This means creating a business that operates without needing your constant involvement in every business process. When you hire employees or implement automation, you will relieve yourself of many of the day-to-day activities.

- You shouldn't be making every sales call as your business grows (heck, we're hiring sales apprentices right now, and we already have a few on the team. Growth is good.)

- You shouldn't be the one developing all your marketing campaigns as your business grows
- You shouldn't be on the phone talking to customers for hours as your company grows

The Hard Work of Creating a Good Work-Life Balance

When you hear about CEOs playing golf during the day or going on the week(s) long vacations, remember that they're afforded the ability to do so because others are handling the day-to-day responsibilities. They likely worked very hard to get to the place where they could have this kind of flexibility.

How do you afford yourself the ability to enjoy the fruits of your labor with your family and friends?

If you truly want to spend more time with your family and friends, you will have to transition from being a business owner (a person who manages and works in their business) to being an entrepreneur—a person who solely oversees the growth of their business.

There is no substitute for hard work in entrepreneurship, and hard work requires a lot of your time and attention. But you didn't become an entrepreneur just to work 24/7 on your business. You became an entrepreneur to have the financial freedom to enjoy life.

As fellow entrepreneurs, we expect each other to work very hard to build successful businesses, but we also want each other to be healthy, well-rounded people who enjoy life and those who are most important to us.

How To Achieve Work-Life Balance as a Father

No doubt that when you become a father, life gets a little more complicated. You were already trying to balance your work, relationship, and friends. Now you have a child. You may even have a couple of them. So how do you balance it all? How do you make it all work? Well we will go over some tips to help you achieve work-life balance.

As a dad, you could have many roles;

- You're a father
- You're a husband or boyfriend
- You're a son to your parents

- You could be a brother
- You are an employee or business owner
- You are a friend

and the list goes on and on

You have all of these roles and you want to be great at all of them. But here's the reality check: You can't be great at all of them all the time. You can't, it's impossible.

You might be a really good father one day, but you didn't pay attention to your wife. or you killed it at work that week, but you ended up not spending much time with your family. You have been taking care of aging parent, but your work has suffered. But I want to be great at all of these things, all the time. This is a problem called WANT IT ALL I know this …..because I suffer from it. WANT IT ALL is a huge epidemic.

I will share a couple of tips to help you achieve a work-life balance.

1. **Be very clear about what you want**. You have to have an honest conversation with yourself. Where do you want to achieve "success"? Do you want a really strong family? or Is your career your #1 priority? It's all ok and there is no judgment, you just have to be clear about it.

Once you are clear then we have the second tip:

2. **Match your actions with what you want**. For example, if your family is your priority, are your actions matching that? or do you tell yourself and everyone else that family is so important, yet you spend time doing a lot of things that don't involve building the family relationship.

3. **Reduce wasted time**: For anyone who says they don't have time…are you watching television? do you spend time on social media? You might be surprised how much time you can gain by dropping those activities. But do I have to watch my shows or play my games? Well, then you might have to go back to tip #1 again and start over.

4. **Improve your scheduling** – If you feel like you need to step up your game in an area of your life, put it on the calendar. That could be a date with your wife or spending time with your child. We put appointments in our work calendar, we can do the same with our personal calendar, It all depends on what your priorities are.

5. **Change your perspective** – Instead of calling it work-life balance, let's call it work-life harmony. Balance feels like you have to give something up to get something else. I think the word harmony is better because it means that everything has to work together. You can work hard and still make time for your family. You can be a good son and take care of your parents, while also making some plans with your friends. As I said in the beginning, you just can't be perfect at all of them all the time. Cut yourself some slack and be careful of how much expectations you are putting on yourself. Your WANT IT ALL problem is your issue and only you can fix it.

CHAPTER FIVE

GOALS OF ENTREPRENEURSHIP TO SET FOR YOURSELF AND YOUR BUSINESS

Goals are an important element when making decisions for a business or measuring progress. They are especially important for entrepreneurs who are starting a business from the beginning. If you're an entrepreneur, you may be looking for some ideas for the types of goals to set yourself. Lets talk about 14 common goals of entrepreneurship and why you may want to set the same goal.

What are Entrepreneurship Goals?

Entrepreneurship goals are goals set by someone who has started a business. These goals are either for the business or for the entrepreneur. They give the entrepreneur something to work toward, which helps them make decisions while they are creating their business. Specific goals also help an entrepreneur track their progress.

Goals of Entrepreneurship

Below are 14 common goals for entrepreneurs and their businesses:

✓ **Develop a Business Plan**

A business plan helps an entrepreneur focus their actions and gives them a goal to work toward. Business plans detail things such as:

- Your business's mission statement
- Your products or services
- Financial information
- Employee information
- Plans for growth

Business plans help entrepreneurs plan out their business before they get started. This makes it a good first goal for entrepreneurs.

✓ Launch Your First Product

Launching your first product is a major milestone for any entrepreneur. It often takes many hours of preparation and works to create that first product. It is your first product that will begin to bring in revenue, an essential element for any new business. Decide what you want your first product to be, how much you plan to sell it for, and how you're going to sell it.

✓ Create an Online Presence

Regardless of the type of business, you're starting, an online presence allows you to reach more people. An online presence typically includes elements such as a website, an email contact address, and social media activity. A common goal for entrepreneurs is to establish an online presence early so that they can begin to attract a wider audience. You can start by creating a website for your new business.

✓ Achieve Financial Stability

Financial stability occurs when a new business is bringing in enough revenue to support itself. Many entrepreneurs fund their ventures primarily through savings. Therefore, an ideal goal is to be able to run your business off of the revenue it is generating rather than using your savings. This is the first step before your business begins to generate a profit.

✓ Hire the Right People

Many entrepreneurs have the goal of growing to the point where they need to hire additional help. This is seen as a sign of strong growth and allows the entrepreneur to delegate some of their responsibilities. If you're setting goals for your new business, consider making one of them hiring the right people. This means you're not only hiring new people for your business, but you're hiring people that will continue to help the business grow. New hires can also bring their positive attributes to the business.

✓ Delegate Effectively

It's important to not only hire the right people but also delegate your responsibilities to them effectively. Many entrepreneurs take on too much responsibility. By delegating key tasks, entrepreneurs can improve the efficiency of their business and their enjoyment from working for the company.

To delegate effectively, entrepreneurs need to go through each of their current responsibilities and decide which ones are more suitable for someone else on their team. They can determine this by analyzing the strengths of their team members and looking at their past work experience before choosing how to reassign important tasks.

✓ Work with Ideal Clients

One of the great things about working as an entrepreneur is that you often get to pick who you work with. However, when you're first starting, you may be less judicious about your clients to generate more revenue. A worthy goal for entrepreneurs is to get to the point where they can work only with their ideal clients. For example, they can choose to work on projects that interest them the most or with companies that have similar values. Working with your ideal clients often makes work more enjoyable and rewarding.

✓ Connect with Like-minded Individuals

Some entrepreneurs who primarily work alone often seek out connections to other entrepreneurs. Developing a network with like-minded individuals provides entrepreneurs with a few benefits. First, it gives you people to talk to who also have a passion for building their own business. Second, you can receive feedback and advice from this network and use it to improve your new business. It's for this reason that some entrepreneurs make it a goal to meet new people who also have an interest in entrepreneurship.

✓ Establish a Brand Identity

A brand identity is the visible elements of your business that provide a specific feeling or impression in an audiences' mind. Establishing a specific brand identity allows a new business to differentiate itself from other businesses in the same market. Entrepreneurs first identify the visible elements of their business that they want to control, such as its color scheme, logo, and tone of voice. Then they modify these elements to better represent the desired brand image and continue to do so until their brand's identity is firmly established within their audience.

✓ Implement a Marketing Strategy

A strong marketing strategy helps a business grow its reach and sell its products. Every new business uses a marketing strategy to grow. The design and implementation of a marketing strategy, therefore, becomes an early goal common for entrepreneurs.

The launching of an email marketing campaign or social media advertising campaign is a significant milestone for a young company.

✓ Find a Healthy Work/Life Balance

Another important milestone for entrepreneurs is when they can have a healthy balance between the amount of time they spend on work and free time. When first starting, many entrepreneurs lack free time because they are spending most of it working on their business. Once they can grow their business to a point where it doesn't need as much attention, the entrepreneur can take more time to relax.

✓ Maintain Steady Business Growth

Entrepreneurs like when they can predict how much their business will grow over a certain amount of time. This makes it easier to make decisions for the business, such as how much they can afford to invest in different areas. It's for this reason that entrepreneurs will aim to have steady business growth, rather than large fluctuations from month to month. To do this, they may implement strategies within the business designed to reduce variations such as standardizing project management techniques.

✓ Focus on Personal Growth

Besides focusing on the growth of the business, some entrepreneurs also make it a goal to focus on personal growth. For example, they may want to learn a new skill or obtain a new professional certification. Sometimes these skills can directly benefit the business, such as learning new software, and other times are just for personal enjoyment, like learning a new language.

✓ Research New Tools and Methods

If an entrepreneur learns of a tool or method that could benefit their business, they may make it a goal to research it. For example, there may be a new project management tool for sale or a better way to handle customer service requests. The entrepreneur researches this new tool or method and determines whether it would improve their business.

The 5 Golden Rules of Goal-Setting

It's called hard work because it is hard. If it were easy, everyone would do it.

As entrepreneurs, we dream of being our own boss, breaking away from corporate restrictions, and pursuing our passion as a business venture. We work long hours, often sacrificing family time and other obligations to do what we feel is in our blood. Being an entrepreneur isn't for everyone, but once we start on that journey, we're not turning back -- no matter how bumpy the road gets.

If being an entrepreneur is your goal, congrats. Now, what? Start writing down your goals. Having a target, or milestones, to reach becomes critical in your ability to achieve more. In fact, 21 percent of goal-setting, high-achieving organizations looked at in one study were more productive than their counterparts, according to Workboard. From the same source: 69 percent of companies surveyed said that communication business goals are the most effective way to build a high-performance team.

However, when you are in business for yourself, there's no one to hold you accountable or keep you on track. You are now that person; therefore, you must be disciplined enough to follow through in every aspect.

Goals are a way to measure your level of success -- they give you focus, direction, and a sense of purpose while providing you a tangible benchmark to determine if you're actually succeeding.

How do any of us define success? It's a relative term. For some of us, it's about how much money they can make. For others, it's about how they're moving the needle forward, how many sales leads they have or the number of media interviews they can get. For me, it all starts with the conditions I've set for achieving my own definition of "satisfaction": the ability to make money, grow professionally and have fun doing it.

Entrepreneurs often set expectations incredibly high and the goals they set are designed to match those lofty expectations. But how do we entrepreneurs know if the goals we're setting for ourselves are realistic and even attainable?

The answer is, know the five golden rules of goal-setting.

1. Set Goals that Motivate You

When you set a goal, it has to mean something, and there has to be value to achieving it. If the outcome is of little to no importance to you, then the chances of your putting in the work are next to none. In fact, 93 percent of people can't translate goals into actions if the goals are irrelevant to them.

So, start with the goals that are highest on your priority list. It's easy to be overwhelmed by everything that needs to be done, so start simple. We live in a "snack-sized" world, meaning that we can digest information in short bites and shut down when we receive too much.

Break down your goals into your top three, or top five, overall goals, the ones with the highest sense of urgency. If it helps, write down why they're valuable to you. I sometimes write these goals down because, a) the list becomes a tangible reminder of what needs to be done; and b) I need the visual aids to help me focus. As every entrepreneur knows, we have a lot of things on our minds, so there's nothing wrong with having a little help.

2. Set SMART Goals.

You may have heard of these already, but it's always useful to have a refresher. If you haven't heard about this acronym, here's what it stands for:

- Specific
- Measurable
- Attainable
- Relevant
- Time-bound

Specific. Your goals need to be as specific as possible because otherwise, they won't give you enough direction to follow through. According to a research paper from the American Psychological Association, setting specific goals led to a higher performance 90 percent of the time for companies studied. Goals are like a lamp lighting the way-- the brighter the light, the clearer the road ahead.

Few business acquaintances were asked about how they set goals and received a response from Jason Forrest, CEO of Forrest Performance Group said, "If you don't have clearly defined goals, you procrastinate. Think about the results you want to achieve -- what activities do you need to do for the results?"

Measurable. Give yourself realistic deadlines to finish the task at hand. Adding specific dates, amounts, etc., makes your progress quantifiable. For example, instead of saying "Reduce expenses," say something like, "Reduce expenses by 10 percent in the next 12 months." That gives you a fixed amount, a time frame to complete your goal and visualize a finish line.

Attainable. Be honest with yourself. As Chowly co-founder Justin McNally said, "'Increase marketing budget by 50 percent in three months' sounds like a great goal, but not a very realistic one. If you're a one-man shop or don't have the resources to do that, you'll only end up frustrated." Instead, he said, "Set realistic and manageable goals. Decide what you want to accomplish in a day and stop when you're done."

Relevant. Align your goals with the direction you want your life and career to take. Balancing the alignment between long-term and short-term will give you the focus you'll need.

Time-bound. Having a finish line will mean you'll get to celebrate when you accomplish your goal. Having set deadlines gives you a sense of urgency that is lacking when goals are open-ended.

3. Write Down your Goals.

I start every day by writing down a list of "to-dos," as well as printing out a calendar with my meetings for the day. I keep these daily goals visible at all times and cross-check the things I've accomplished to gauge where I stand at the end of the day. This is a best practice for me because it makes things tangible and me accountable.

Your own long-term goals don't have to be spelled out quite as publicly, but you should keep them someplace where, every so often, you are reminded of where you want to go. Use an active voice when writing them down; for example, say, "I will increase my marketing budget." Using more passive language such as "I would like..." gives you an excuse to get sidetracked.)

4. Put a Plan in Action.

It's easy to get so focused on the outcome that you forget the steps needed to achieve the outcome. You might go from A through Z, giving little thought to B, C, D, and everything in between. So, write down all of the individual steps. This is your road map to executing your plan as flawlessly as possible.

Harry Mills, CEO of The Aha! Advantage and author of Zero Resistance said: "Successful entrepreneurs map out their goals to achieve them. Entrepreneurs that develop a map to reach an achievement or overcome indecision are compelled to take action." Along the way, seek out the advice of your peers -- a former business partner, a trusted advisor, or mentor. They might have insights you've overlooked.

5. Work on the Plan.

Having a plan in place makes you official. Working on the plan makes you successful. If you take the time to draw up a good plan, why not use it? It's tempting to keep changing your mind or to draw new plans when things go awry, but variables aren't an excuse not to stick to the plan. Trust your instincts.

One important piece of advice I've given is: Look long-term but live short-term. It's really easy to think about the things you want and the money you can make, but those don't become possible without the here and now.

Don't get ahead of yourself. Trust your plan, work the plan, be flexible when handling variables and you'll get there. It's called hard work because it is hard. If it were easy, everyone would do it.

CHAPTER SIX

ENTREPRENEURIAL MINDSET - WAYS TO THINK LIKE AN ENTREPRENEUR

It took me a long time to develop an entrepreneurial mindset.

Honestly, I feel like I spent most of my early 20s trying to undo the mindset I was taught in school – you know, "get good grades, fall into line, get a good job…"

But what about entrepreneurship?

Looking back, it frustrates me how my teachers were so concerned with students getting good jobs, but never even mentioned the possibility that we could start a business instead.

This is even more frustrating when you consider where most jobs come from. People who decide to carve their own path, start a business, and employ others…

What gives?

After a few years of trying – and many failed businesses – I finally learned how to think like an entrepreneur.

The payoff? Good money, fun work, constant travel, and freedom. Not bad, right?

If you want to learn how to develop an entrepreneurial mindset so you can build a successful business, you're reading the right book. In this, we'll explore 20 essential entrepreneurial mindset characteristics.

But first, what does it mean to have an entrepreneurial mindset, and why is it important?

What is an Entrepreneurial Mindset?

An entrepreneurial mindset is a set of beliefs, thought processes, and ways of viewing the world that drives entrepreneurial behavior. Typically, entrepreneurs firmly believe it's possible to improve their life situation and live life on their own terms. They also believe in their ability to learn, grow, adapt, and succeed.

The mindset of successful entrepreneurs is different from the mindset of traditional workers in many ways.

For example, if a traditional worker needs to earn more money, they'll often brush up their resume and look for a better-paid job. However, someone with an entrepreneurial mindset would look for ways to earn money by starting or growing a business.

Here's the thing: Anyone can develop the mindset of a successful entrepreneur. As the founder of Ford Motor Company, Henry Ford once said, "Whether you think you can or think you can't – you're right."

The Importance of an Entrepreneurial Mindset

The power of an entrepreneurial mindset is obvious when you think about it. Entrepreneurs succeed like they do because they think, act, and view the world differently from most people.

There are so many reasons why an entrepreneurial mindset matters. For example, developing an entrepreneurial mindset can help to reduce doubt, fear, and anxiety. It can also help to drive action, focus, and growth.

In short, an entrepreneurial mentality is the foundation of business success. Now, let's explore how entrepreneurs think.

How to Think Like an Entrepreneur: 20 Entrepreneurial Mindset Characteristics

If you want to learn how to build an entrepreneurial mindset, you need to know how successful entrepreneurs think. So, let's take a closer look at 20 essential entrepreneurial mindset characteristics. Entrepreneurs are:

1. Independent

This is one of the most important aspects of the entrepreneurial mindset.

Entrepreneurs don't follow the crowd or look to others to be given instructions. Instead, they listen to their gut and carve their own path.

As Apple's founder, Steve Jobs, said, "Don't let the noise of others' opinions drown out your own inner voice."

2. Responsible

The independent mindset of successful entrepreneurs stems from taking full responsibility.

Entrepreneurs don't blame others for their life situation – they empower themselves by taking responsibility for improving it.

Failure, success, life circumstances – it doesn't matter what it is. Even if something isn't your fault, by taking responsibility for it, you're empowered to improve it.

3. Abundant

A key part of the entrepreneurial mindset is abundance.

Entrepreneurs know they can improve a situation, make more money, and create new opportunities.

The sky is always the limit.

As a result, entrepreneurs don't hoard money or knowledge. They're open, generous, and understand that "you get what you give."

The author and entrepreneur Robert Kiyosaki once wrote, "I have never met a rich person who has never lost any money. But I have met a lot of poor people who have never lost a dime."

4. Goal-Oriented

Entrepreneurial thinking is goal-orientated.

In other words, successful entrepreneurs don't have wishes and dreams – they have goals and plans.

So, when creating an entrepreneurial mindset, set SMART goals – goals that are:

- Specific
- Measurable
- Attainable
- Relevant
- Time-sensitive

5. Not Afraid of Failure

When learning how to think like an entrepreneur, you need to look at failure differently from most people.

Entrepreneurs don't fear failure – they appreciate it.

Each "failure" is simply a stepping stone to learn from, helping to move you closer to success. As the famous inventor, Thomas Edison said, "I have not failed. I've just found 10,000 ways that won't work."

Failing at something certainly doesn't mean that you're a failure – just that something didn't work out as you'd hoped, and you need to try again.

6. Growth-Oriented

Stanford University psychologist Dr. Carol Dweck studied failure and said, "For 20 years, my research has shown that the view you adopt for yourself profoundly affects the way you lead your life."

Specifically, she found that there are two main types of mindset: fixed and growth.

Someone with a fixed mindset believes that who they are is relatively permanent and can't change very much.

The entrepreneur mindset is growth-oriented.

Entrepreneurs believe that they can grow as people, learn new things, and develop new skills. They believe that – with some consistent effort – they can shape themselves into whoever they want to be.

The best-selling author and entrepreneur Hal Elrod said, "Your level of success will rarely exceed your level of personal development because success is something you attract by the person you become."

In other words, personal growth tends to create success. So, keep trying to improve yourself.

7. Feedback-Seeking

The most successful entrepreneurs aren't worried about looking cool – they just want to succeed, and they know that learning from feedback will help speed up the process.

Dr. Carol S. Dweck said, "Why waste time proving over and over how great you are when you could be getting better?"

In short, don't look for validation, seek feedback.

8. Learning-Oriented

Most people spend their spare time seeking entertainment, whether it's social media, Netflix, gaming, reading novels, or hanging with friends.

However, entrepreneurial thinking is more concerned with learning and development. For example:

Instead of watching TV, entrepreneurs may take an online course to help them move toward their goals.

Instead of gaming, entrepreneurs will often spend hours tweaking their sales funnel.

And instead of scrolling through social media, entrepreneurs are more likely to listen to motivational podcasts or read business books.

As the entrepreneur and speaker Jim Rohn said, "Formal education will make you a living; self-education will make you a fortune."

9. Forward-Thinking

If you want to learn how to think like an entrepreneur, you need to think long-term.

The famous billionaire investor Warren Buffett said, "Someone is sitting in the shade today because someone planted a tree a long time ago."

Successful entrepreneurs know that big goals take a long time to achieve. So, they start with their goal and work backward, reverse-engineering every step of the way. In other words, "If I want this, I need to do that. But to do that, I need to do this," and so on.

They keep working and are patient when it comes to rewards – they know that the tortoise always beats the hare.

10. Self-Accepting

Many people struggle with self-acceptance. When you don't like something about yourself, it's easy to devalue or even hate yourself.

But if you develop a growth mindset, you know you can always change and improve.

So, successful entrepreneurs accept themselves as they are, warts and all. They know who they are is transient, and they're working on becoming the person they want to be.

11. Self-Aware

Entrepreneurs know that the only thing holding us back is our-selves (because they take full responsibility, remember!)

As a result, they practice self-awareness.

They pay close attention to their strengths and weaknesses, which allows them to improve faster and play to their strengths.

12. Collaborative

Great businesses require teamwork – after all, Jeff Bezos didn't build Amazon alone. So, if you want to think like an entrepreneur, you need to think in terms of "we" instead of "I."

There's an African proverb that says, "If you want to go fast, go alone. If you want to go far, go together."

As a result, successful entrepreneurs think collaboratively and practice their leadership skills.

13. Courageous

It's not easy to start a business.

As the famous management consultant Peter Drucker said, "Whenever you see a successful business, someone once made a courageous decision."

But this doesn't mean that entrepreneurs aren't afraid.

Nelson Mandela, the activist and former president of South Africa, explains, "I learned that courage was not the absence of fear, but the triumph over it."

14. Comfortable with Discomfort

Courage leads to an essential entrepreneurial mindset characteristic: learning to be comfortable with discomfort.

Growth and expansion require you to move beyond your comfort zone. So, when developing an entrepreneurial mindset, practice leaning into uncomfortable situations, such as rejection.

For example, after realizing his fear of rejection was holding him back, the entrepreneur and keynote speaker Jia Jiang spent 100 days getting rejected on purpose!

15. Adaptable

Entrepreneurs have big goals, and they know it's impossible to see the entire staircase before climbing. But they climb anyway, safe in the knowledge that they can always adapt to new developments.

For example, if your first product fails, try another one. And if your Facebook ads still don't generate sales, hone your skills.

16. Problem-Solving

Entrepreneurs look for problems and try to find ways to solve them.

If you think about it, this is the essence of every business. For instance, plumbers fix broken pipes, Netflix cures boredom, and car manufacturers help people get around.

Brian Chesky, the co-founder of Airbnb, said, "If we tried to think of a good idea, we wouldn't have been able to think of a good idea. You just have to find the solution for a problem in your own life."

17. Driven and Tenacious

Drive is an essential part of the entrepreneurial mind. Entrepreneurs are self-motivated and driven to achieve their goals. They work hard and enjoy the ride, knowing that they'll reap the rewards down the line.

The entrepreneur Mark Cuban said, "It's not about money or connections. It's the willingness to outwork and outlearn everyone when it comes to your business."

Similarly, entrepreneurs set out to achieve their goals come hell or high water. When the going gets tough, they stick with it – they don't give up.

As Henry Ford, founder of Ford Motor Company, said, "When everything seems to be going against you, remember that the airplane takes off against the wind, not with it."

18. Focused

Successful entrepreneurs are focused on achieving their goals. They're focused, never procrastinate, and always prioritize the most important tasks.

To do this, ask yourself, "Will this help me to achieve my long-term goals?" If the answer is yes, then ask, "Is this the most important thing to do right now?"

19. Action-Oriented

"Wantrepreneurs" like to read books, watch videos, and make plans – but they never actually get down to business and work.

Entrepreneurs have a bias for action. They know that knowledge without action is meaningless. As the entrepreneur, Walt Disney said, "The way to get started is to quit talking and begin doing."

20. Decisive

The entrepreneurial mind is decisive.

Entrepreneurs must confront problems and make many decisions every day – often with inadequate information to help.

Successful entrepreneurs decide and then get back to work. They know that "you can always edit a bad page. You can't edit a blank page," as the author Jodi Picoult said.

So practice decisiveness – for example, next time you're in a restaurant, look at the menu once, decide, and order with confidence.

Summary: How to Develop an Entrepreneurial Mindset

Having an entrepreneurial mindset will allow you to think, act, and perceive the world differently from the average worker, setting the foundation for success.

Now, you can't develop an entrepreneurial mindset overnight.

But, by understanding some key entrepreneurial mindset characteristics, you can watch your behavior and learn how to think like an entrepreneur. In summary, here are 20 entrepreneurial mindset traits:

- Independent
- Responsible
- Abundant
- Goal-oriented
- Not afraid of failure
- Growth-oriented
- Feedback-seeking
- Learning-oriented
- Forward-thinking
- Self-accepting
- Self-aware
- Collaborative
- Courageous
- Comfortable with discomfort
- Adaptable
- Problem-solving

- Driven and tenacious
- Focused
- Action-oriented
- Decisive

CHAPTER SEVEN

HOW TO HANDLE FAILURE AS AN ENTREPRENEUR

In business, failure is almost inevitable; especially for start-ups as they are usually handled by newbies in the business world; bound to make a whole lot of mistakes. There are ways a business could fail ranging from raising funds, sales to managing the business altogether. What is more important is the attitude of entrepreneurs towards handling failure.

A lot of the successful entrepreneurs came out stronger after a series of huge failures. For instance, Oprah Winfrey who was fired from a news channel for "being unfit for TV" is now the Queen of Daytime Talk TV and a billionaire. Henry Ford didn't let failed businesses and bankruptcy stop him from building one of the most successful car companies in the world. If you don't give up, you can be successful like these people.

Here's how to deal with failure:

✓ **Prepare Yourself**

"The reality is, sometimes you lose. And you are never too good to lose, you are never too big to lose, you are never too smart to lose, it happens. And it happens when it needs to happen. And you have to embrace these things." Beyoncé

Failure is bound to happen at one point or another, so face reality and prepare yourself for the worst. You might think that your product is the best and a lot of consumers need it, but the launch strategy is a mess and nobody is buying. You have practically failed in that aspect. In business, there are 50% chances of winning and 50% chances of losing. By preparing yourself, you won't be caught unawares, rather you face it with a determination to succeed. Running away from it will only lead to hundreds of failures.

✓ Be Positive

Successful entrepreneurs have a positive mindset; they always see the good in every negative situation and failure. They do not say to themselves, "I am a failure", rather they find ways of turning a failure to be a massive success. And that is what sets them apart from failed entrepreneurs.

✓ Don't Take it Personal

We all have different ways of handling rejection or failure. So, when you experience a failure in your business, don't go about feeling sorry for yourself or lamenting how you have failed yourself and those that believe in you. The fact that you have failed does not mean you are a total failure or you can't try again and succeed. Rather take it as a learning process, where you learn from your failure and grow.

If you take it too personal, you will find yourself wallowing in your sorrow and pain. And the time you spend doing that can be put into preparing yourself for your comeback. The choice is all yours.

✓ Take Responsibility

Blaming someone else for your failure won't make you feel better, so hold yourself accountable for every misstep that leads to the failure of your business. Retrace your steps and avoid making the same mistakes in the future.

At this stage, figure out your strengths and weaknesses in business and work on the latter.

✓ Analyze the Situation

"It is fine to celebrate success, but it is more important to heed the lessons of failure. How a company deals with mistakes suggests how well it will bring out the best ideas and talents of its people, how effectively it will respond to change."

Bill Gates

By analyzing the situation, you are re-evaluating your business by trying to figure out what you did and didn't do. Finding answers to why your business failed at first attempt or severally as the case may be; what went wrong, how it could have been prevented. By doing this, you are taking notes of the lesson for your previous business failure and building on those lessons to remodel.

    ✓   **Start again**

"I have not failed 10,000 times, I have not failed once. I have succeeded in proving that those 10,000 ways will not work. When I have eliminated the ways that will not work, I will find the way that will work."

Thomas Edison.

If only all entrepreneurs could have the positivist spirit as Thomas Edison who tried more than 10,000 times to invent a light bulb. I must say, that is really a lot of time to try out a single thing. The lesson of the story is, he didn't give up. He was persistent and he was determined to succeed. With this positivist spirit and motivation, rise and start over.

You could start a whole new business bearing in mind not to repeat the same mistakes you made in the previous one or you could rebrand your business with a complete model hoping it would work.

Without failure, you don't get to learn and grow outside your comfort zone. Failure is a setback preparing you for your grand comeback. And without failure, there may not be a success story. So embrace your failures and rejection, learn from them and soar higher.

"The business empires built by successful entrepreneurs were erected on the foundation of past failures."

Ajaero Tony Martins.

All Entrepreneurs Fail: How to Use Failure to Your Advantage

All entrepreneurs fail.

Let that sink in.

All entrepreneurs fail.

If you're an entrepreneur, at some point you will fail. It's inevitable. Whether that failure is large or small, there's something to be gained.

Failure is often considered the other "F" word in the startup and entrepreneur sector, but it shouldn't be.

Failure isn't an all-out loss — you can use failure to your advantage.

Entrepreneurs aren't the only ones to fail, either. Forty percent of all businesses will fail in the first three years they're open. That's a lot of failing businesses.

For entrepreneurs, the risk is even higher. Entrepreneurs intentionally begin their businesses to disrupt an industry. This raises their risk of falling on their faces.

Furthermore, the longer a business is around, the more likely it is to fail at some point.

The riskiest period for a new business is the first 3-5 years, where you can see that there's a sharp decline in the number of businesses.

Successful people fail. And no, that's not an oxymoron.

The following are ways entrepreneurs can use failure as their advantage:

> **Failure is an Option**

Failure is often viewed as an ending, but that doesn't have to be the case. For most entrepreneurs and their businesses, failure is just the beginning.

If you find your business failing, it's time to pivot and find a solution to the problem. Just know that failure is an option.

Maybe you need to start over from scratch. If so, that's OK. My own first business failed, but I'm still standing (and then some).

Why? Because I examined the problems with my first business and made sure that what I learned informed my future decisions.

This is especially important for small businesses. One study conducted in Australia found that the size of a business correlated to its survival rate.

Failure is a stepping stone on the pathway to success. You pick up new pieces of information along the way that help you to avoid mistakes.

And businesses fail for lots of reasons. An NSBA study asked participants about the biggest obstacles they faced in terms of keeping their businesses afloat. Nearly half of the respondents felt that economic uncertainty was at the top of the list.

However, you'll also note that only 5 percent of respondents felt they faced no significant challenges.

If you're struggling to stay on your feet, you're not alone.

But here's the thing: You can't control the economy. No one has a magic wand that can guarantee economic growth.

You can't control regulatory boards, either, or the cost of health insurance benefits.

That's why successful entrepreneurs focus on the things they can control.

If you can pivot from your existing direction and find a solution to the problem that's causing your business to fail, your failure will quickly turn into a success and a lesson learned.

> **Accept Failure**

Failure is part of the process of starting a business and being an entrepreneur.

You might hear about lots of "overnight successes." In most cases, these stories don't reveal the missteps behind the eventual achievements.

For instance, researchers and doctors often invent thousands of failed vaccines before they finally make one that works.

Similarly, entrepreneurs sometimes start several businesses before they find a formula that results in profits.

Some business owners, on the other hand, are so scared of failure that they're debilitated with fear. This fear stops them from acting, pivoting, creating, and founding.

If you find that you're scared of failure, try to find acceptance.

As I said before, you're not alone.

There are many reasons that startups fail. According to a poll conducted by CB Insights, business founders stated that their businesses most often failed because of a lack of market need.

In other words, businesses often go under because the founders neglected to conduct some basic market research. And you know how I feel about data-driven decisions.

If nearly half of businesses break down because there's no need for the products or services they provide, there's an easy way to reverse the trend.

Entrepreneurs can automatically learn from these failures and conduct the proper research before they ever launch their businesses.

It's common sense, but many entrepreneurs are so in love with their ideas that they don't consider the other side of the equation.

The second most common reason behind businesses that flop boils down to cold, hard cash. Almost 30 percent of business owners reported that their businesses never took off because they ran out of money.

Inadequate cash flow could trace back to lots of causes.

Maybe the business didn't collect on accounts receivable aggressively enough.

Perhaps the business failed to leverage PPC ads correctly.

Whatever the case, there's almost always a reason behind the reason. If you can accept failure and learn from it, you'll know how to avoid making the same mistake twice.

> **Be Honest**

Let's say that your business or a specific product doesn't work out. In the startup world, you have to be honest with your team.

If your company is beginning to lose momentum, or if you've made some grievous error, own up to it.

Entrepreneurs often feel alone in building their business and alone in their failure. But you're not. Your team and your partners are behind you whether you're successful or falling apart.

The sooner that you can admit to them that there is a problem, the more likely they are to want to help you solve the problem and stick it out to make the business successful.

Lots of entrepreneurs and business owners feel uncertain about their future.

If you don't admit to your failure, someone else will eventually point it out. If someone else has to point out your failure or mistake, it's going to look a lot worse.

It's much better to be upfront and honest when you make an error or even if you run your business into the ground.

Of course, you also have to be honest with yourself.

Don't lie to yourself that there isn't a problem when you know that there is one. Catching a failure early can mean you've got plenty of time to turn it around.

The alternative means a big mess on your hands.

➢ Answer Questions

If you've failed in some way, it's not only your skin in the game — it's your team's. After you've admitted to your failure, you can offer explanations, but not excuses.

If you own up to the failure and examine it publicly, you can learn more about what went wrong.

Furthermore, part of examining your failure is asking and answering questions. You should also feel comfortable answering any questions that your team might have.

Instead of hiding in your office, call a team meeting. Instead of pretending that you're raking in the dough, show your team a profit-and-loss sheet.

Your honesty and willingness to answer questions will also build a stronger team mentality. From that point, you can rebuild.

Startup companies are naturally resilient in the face of failure as they're lean and can easily change direction. This gives them some advantages over larger companies and the potential to even beat out the bigger competition.

➢ Deal with your Emotions

There's a big difference between a reaction and a response.

A reaction is your emotional, knee-jerk response. A reaction usually exacerbates the problem.

This is because business is not emotional. The stock market doesn't care whether or not you make money. Neither do consumers.

An emotional reaction leads to a lack of movement and action.

A response, on the other hand, implies inertia.

For example, if you know that your leads aren't converting, you can adjust your marketing funnel to bring in lost prospects.

Similarly, if you know that your products don't resonate with consumers, you can go back to R&D.

By examining and dealing with your emotions, you'll be more likely to have the ability to respond to a failure instead of reacting to it.

Dealing with your emotions doesn't mean just checking them at the door. Failure can make entrepreneurs feel angry, sad, scared, and any number of other emotions.

Examine those emotions. Take some time to process what has happened and then come up with a plan on how to make positive changes.

➢ Learn

It's as simple as that: Learn from your failure. No matter the failure, there's always some insight for you to glean from the experience.

A major part of turning failure to your advantage is learning how and why the failure happened.

Not learning from your failure opens the door to future failures. You might miss the mark often as an entrepreneur.

However, if you don't seize the opportunity to grow and rebuild, you'll miss out on all the great parts of running your own business.

Start from the drawing board. Come up with a new idea. Get excited about something that you're passionate about.

Knowing that many new businesses fail keeps many people from starting their own companies.

Don't let potential failure deter you from realizing your dreams. Instead, embrace an uncertain future and know that failure is a possible outcome.

> ➢ **Plan for the Future**

Part of learning from your failure is creating a plan for the future. Making the same mistake twice means that you didn't learn from your error.

Almost 30 percent of businesses fail from a lack of funding. Many receive funding from outside sources, but 79 percent of small businesses with fewer than 5 employees also use their own savings — and that's declining.

Your plan will shift and change as time passes, but not having a plan is a failure by itself.

For instance, I'm known for creating complex content marketing plans. I never launch a campaign unless I know exactly where I'm going.

Furthermore, I don't create a plan without first diving into the data. What has worked for other companies? What has worked for me before?

When I know this information, I can not only create a plan, but I can also execute it. And I don't have to rely on raw faith.

Planning for the future allows you to have extra capital, an exit plan, and a strong team that can anticipate potential problems and maintain strong momentum.

> ➢ **Get Motivated**

Turn the anxious energy a failure creates into motivation.

Failure is just one step on a very long journey to entrepreneurial success. Use the failure to motivate you into making your business a success instead of scaring you into submission.

Failure coupled with fear can mean the end of your business. Failure coupled with motivation leads to success.

If you need to find your motivation during times of failure, just hear the voices of all the people who said you couldn't do it. Then get back up and keep going.

➢ Gain Perspective

Similar to using failure to give you motivation, use your failure to gain perspective.

Failure means that you've done something. If you had never started a business, you couldn't be failing at it. Use that perspective to approach your future goals and obstacles.

Your failure can show you where your weaknesses are.

Examine your failure to find out your business's weak spots.

Have you struggled to generate brand awareness? Do your customers have trouble finding you online?

Once you've identified those weak spots, you can test new ideas. I'm a big fan of creating a hypothesis and testing it in real life.

If you're not sure how to gain perspective on your failure, ask for help. Asking an outside source or mentor to examine your business when there is a failure can help gain perspective.

Gaining perspective might not happen right away. Processing a failure, ridding yourself of your emotions, and finding your logical reasoning can take time.

Once you're able to think logically, you'll be able to gain the perspective that you need to turn your failed business idea around.

➢ Discover the Positive

So many of these tips lead right here: Find the positive.

Failure can be emotional, especially when your business is like your child. That type of failure can be debilitating for any entrepreneur.

Checking your emotions, examining your failure, and taking the time to gain perspective will help you to find the positive aspects of the problem.

Looking for the silver lining in a failure can help you to refocus your mind on the problem. Turning failure to your advantage is simple when you can see why that failure is positive or may benefit your business.

The silver lining will depend upon your failure. Your failure might help you to spot the weaknesses in your business and fix them. Your failure might help you to identify a team member who doesn't fit the company.

When my first business failed, I paved the path toward success with Crazy Egg, Hello Bar, and other initiatives.

No matter the problem, look for something positive. If you stay stuck in the negative, you'll never manage to move forward.

> **Don't get Burned Out**

Entrepreneurs sometimes feel like hamsters on those little plastic wheels. They keep running in circles, but they don't get anywhere.

Don't let your business's failure burn you out.

Burnout is very common in the entrepreneurial world. Startups require long hours and full commitment from their founders. Working at these levels makes it easy to exhaust your resources.

Instead of continuing on the hamster wheel, pause for a moment and assess your direction. Repeating the same action over and over again won't change the outcome.

When you're stuck, try the exact opposite approach. Many entrepreneurs discover their best ideas when they reframe the issue and consider alternative paths.

A major stressor for many startups is funding. This is especially true because 73 percent of entrepreneurial businesses start their business with funds from their own personal savings.

By using their own savings, these entrepreneurs are completely invested in their business. It often means that their family members are invested, too.

That's a lot of pressure!

Such deep immersion in your business — both in time and money — makes it easy to burn out if you don't look for the warning signs.

High-stress levels, lack of sleep, and lack of clarity all indicate burnout.

You don't want to lose momentum. You can rise above your failures instead of letting them take you down and ruin your business.

> ➤ **Fail Big**

Go big or go home. That's the mantra for many an entrepreneur.

Myself included.

And that shouldn't apply only to success. If you're starting a new business, dream big and create something huge.

A major failure means that you had the potential for major success. If you're going to fail, you might as well go big.

A big failure can be used to your advantage in the same way that a small failure would. You might just need more time to find the best way forward.

A large failure might mean the end of your current business, but it still doesn't take you out of the game.

I've started lots of companies. Some of them are bigger successes than others. And like I mentioned before, I've failed plenty of times.

Does that mean I resign myself to a life of unrealized dreams? Of course not!

If you fail big, know that you tried big, too.

> ➤ **Learn about Yourself**

We can see our true selves when we fail. Just like failure shows the weaknesses in your business, it can also reveal aspects of your personality that you weren't aware of.

One way to gain perspective on your failure is to take a step back and learn about yourself. Ask yourself these questions:

- How have I reacted to this failure?
- Did I react or respond to the failure?
- What does this failure mean to me and my business?
- How did my team interact and respond while handling this failure?

- What can I do better next time that I find myself in a similar situation?

These questions can help you to examine your failure and to learn more about yourself and how you respond to stressful situations.

One business stressor that can lead to failure is an unexpected expense. A Gallup poll shows that 36 percent of small business owners faced several large, unexpected expenses.

The big one? Costs related to employees.

Unexpected costs can lead to failure for small businesses that are running on a limited budget. If that unexpected cost is related to other team members, that can create another failure: mistrust between colleagues.

Teams need to trust each other to thrive. This is why it's so important for entrepreneurs to own their failures publicly and to lead by example.

> **Fail Quickly**

If you're going to fail, do it quickly. Drawing out a downward slide won't lessen the pain when you finally hit bottom.

Once you know that you're failing, it's time to respond aggressively. The quicker you can adjust your strategy, the faster you can bring about your next success.

How Failure can make you a Better Entrepreneur

Every entrepreneur feels it at some point: The fear of failure. Only half of new businesses make it to their fifth birthday, and that can cause entrepreneurs a lot of stress. However, experts say failure can actually lead to major accomplishments.

In fact, failure has been a key ingredient in some of the business world's great success stories, says Michel Bergeron, BDC's Chief Strategy Officer.

"Canadian entrepreneurs and the public at large need to be more forgiving about failure. "Failure—and learning from mistakes—is often an important milestone on the path to success. We have to change our perception about failure in order to help business owners stay in the game."

I will share thoughts about the role of failure in business success.

✓ Learn, Adapt and Succeed

No business is too big or too small to confront roadblocks. I will cite the example of Groupon, the giant deals website.

The company got its start as a social media site called The Point, which was created to help people connect for social activism purposes. After a year of effort and US$1 million in operating costs, the start-up was going nowhere.

"The founders shifted gears and turned their offering into the discount coupon service Groupon. They learned, adapted, and made a fortune. Two years later, the shift in focus proved profitable. Groupon ballooned from a few dozen employees to 10,000 and was the fastest company in history to make US$1 billion in revenue.

✓ Adopt a "Try, Try Again" Philosophy

It is advised entrepreneurs adopt a "try, try again" philosophy.

Learning from mistakes and showing resiliency is a business approach that's growing in popularity in today's rapidly changing economy.

Instead of the old model, which emphasized extensive planning before launching a new venture—by which time technology and markets may change substantially—the new approach favors a lean and nimble approach.

The idea is to engage customers early with a basic product, even if you haven't worked out all the bugs. Learn quickly from customer feedback and missteps. And then constantly refine your efforts. The final secret ingredient? Don't give up.

✓ A New Take on Failure

How do entrepreneurs turn failure into success? They have a knack for seeing failure as an opportunity or challenge.

"When solution 'A' didn't work, they tried solution 'B' if they were still convinced there was a need. Or they decided to meet a different need and, in the process, found a new path. The setback helped them identify a weakness, and they fixed it."

Conclusion

All entrepreneurs fail. Myself included.

Successful entrepreneurs use that failure to their advantage.

Failure is not the end of the world. And without failure, there can't be success. If you never become an entrepreneur or start the business that you've been dreaming of, you'll never fail.

But you'll also never succeed.

And the most important part of using failure to your advantage as an entrepreneur is to learn from your mistakes. And from the mistakes of others.

CHAPTER EIGHT

ROLE OF MOTIVATION IN ENTREPRENEURSHIP

Entrepreneurs are known for their tenacity and commitment – to lofty ideals, long hours, and success. They are hard workers who go into a project passionately and find success because they can convince other people of the value of their ideas. A key factor in sustaining this kind of energy, creativity, and drive is motivation. The role of motivation in entrepreneurship is foundational to their ultimate success.

Why is Motivation Important?

Motivation services as the reason, or reasons, that compel someone to continue striving and working. It provides hope and clarity when circumstances become hard and discouraging. Entrepreneurial motivation, then, is fundamental in someone's decision to embark on the journey of creating a business.

Motivation is also important to those that entrepreneurs work with and interact with. Entrepreneurs need to understand, tap into, and sustain their own motivation for starting a business, but they also need to be able to motivate others to buy into their idea. Whether it's motivating investment groups to provide startup funding or motivating eventual employees during the early days, motivation is key to keeping everyone on the same page about the mission of the new business and working towards fulfilling that.

What are Motivational Influences on Entrepreneurship?

Every entrepreneur and business owner is different; therefore, many entrepreneurial motivation factors will also be different. But there are similarities among successful entrepreneurs in where they find motivation and inspiration.

Here are some of the things that not only motivate entrepreneurs to go into business for themselves but keep motivating them to continue even during difficult parts of the process.

- **Greater Freedom**

  Entrepreneurship often appeals to people who want to work for themselves. Whether they no longer want to report to a supervisory structure or simply want to be able to create their own hours, entrepreneurship gives people more freedom and flexibility in how they structure their careers. And while there is an inherent anxiety in entrepreneurship, as there is a lot of unknown about the possible success of a startup, it also can be freeing to know that your employment is secure in the sense that you can define your own parameters of success, salary, and so on.

- **Greater Income**

  Some workers feel that all the work they put into a business owned by someone else ultimately goes to help add to that owner's wealth. While employees receive a salary for their work, they are limited in how much they can earn when compared to C-suite level employees, owners, and shareholders. Starting your own business creates the possibility of increased wealth over time.

- **Greater Influence**

  Relatedly, some employees disapprove of the direction that the company they work for is taking, or they want to have a more direct hand in some part of the business. Wanting to have a greater influence over a product's development, marketing, or customer base is a significant motivator for some people to break away from a business or career path and start their own company or product line. It can also appeal to people who want to have a lasting impact or legacy in an industry, as starting a company sets them apart.

- **Control and Creativity**

  Many entrepreneurs have an idea they want to share with the world or that they think could influence people's lives for the better. Wanting greater creative control over the product and business process is a driving motivation that launches the career of many self-made business people and can help create focus and provide inspiration throughout the entrepreneurial process.

The role of motivation in entrepreneurship is significant. It helps to shape startup businesses from the very early stages and can have an impact on sustaining growth and capabilities into the future.

How to Push Yourself to the Next Level and Achieve Success

Limits are stumbling blocks between you and your success. You will face stiff resistance when attempting to break through the limit. Resistance could be self-inflicted fear, doubt, low self-esteem, physical disabilities, and mental block. These elements could package themselves as huge barriers.

Sadly enough, most people find it hard to push themselves beyond these limits. They eventually give up and accept the status quo.

As long as you desire a life of success, you must face your fear and push yourself beyond the limits. Failure to do this will truncate your dream and make your goals unrealizable.

The 3 Phases of Life

There are three phases of life that we all constantly cycle between – the pushing phase, the overdoing phase, and the relaxation phase.

Pushing yourself or taking it slow may depend on which of the phases you find yourself in. Let's examine the phases in detail.

1. The Pushing Phase

You feel excited about your life, environment, and things in general. You are stepping out of your comfort zone, which many people find hard to do. And this action is also paying off as you are growing.

In this phase, your momentum is high and you may experience exhaustion after using your energy on tasking activities.

2. The Overdoing Phase

At this stage, you are taking on more tasks than you can handle. You are saying 'yes' to every task dole at you. You can't say 'no'. You might even be tense because you feel you miss deadlines on the project.

This is the phase that precedes burnout. Life becomes overwhelming, so this stage requires adequate management, which I will share in the next phase.

3. The Resting Phase

It's time to reflect and regain your balance. If you have been overdoing it while pushing yourself, it is time to rest.

Here is when you ask salient questions such as:

- Am I satisfied with this job?
- Am I working in line with my core values?
- Am I happy in my relationship?'

So, what's the right phase to be in? The truth is there is none.

However, the pushing phase is the ideal place. Life is challenging enough to stay disengaged. It takes pushing yourself to make the best out of the situation you go through in life.

Why Should You Push Yourself?

Knowing all these, you might ask why should you push yourself? Here are 8 reasons to do so.

- **Get Out of Your Comfort Zone**

  Life is boring in a comfort zone. Some people believe you can succeed better in your comfort zone than exploring new frontiers. While that may be true, yet nothing significant can happen until you dare.
  You need to do different things and do things differently. You need to see the world and life from another perspective. You need a different result. You can achieve all these by doing the same thing over and again.
  Life only rewards those who dare and not those who wish.

- **Tap Your Inner Strength**

  If you have never come across a lion in the jungle, you might never get the chance to tap your running potential. Don't wait until something pushes you; push yourself.
  You have untapped strength to overcome any obstacles than you can ever imagine. Use that strength and refuse to live a life of mediocrity and complacency.

- **Learn New Things**

  Until you push yourself, you cannot explore. And it takes exploration to learn new things. Start a new business and open yourself to new opportunities. Whatever you do, ensure you are learning, growing, and pushing yourself.

- **Stay in Shape**

  Pushing yourself also impacts your body. You become fit when you refuse to stay at rest.
  For instance, you can use the step instead of the elevator. Get your body in motion and stay fit, especially in this lockdown(Covid-19 pandemic). Studies have revealed that you burn calories as much as 6 to 15% more when you engage in high-intensity exercises.

- **Achieve More!**

  Past glories produce future rewards. Push yourself to generate more results than you did yesterday. Find out what you can do more, even if it is only 5 minutes more. Anytime you make extra effort to add value to your life or that of others, you learn and grow beyond your limits and strength.

- **Discover Your Identity**

  You don't know your worth and capabilities until you stretch. Listen up! The only competitor you have is YOU! it is while you exert yourself that you get to realize your beliefs, limits, and strengths. Pushing yourself will help you know your true identity.

- **Build Momentum**

  Death occurs in a state of rest. Would you rather be stagnant water or a flowing river? You need sustained momentum to achieve your goals in all aspects of your life. You can build momentum by going the extra mile in achieving your goals.

- **Define Your Limits**

  How do you even know your limits if you don't push yourself? The next time you push yourself, you will realize you can break through those limits.

How Do You Push Yourself Beyond Limits and Achieve Success?

It is easier to stay in a more comfortable zone than to dare or explore new frontiers. Meanwhile, not pushing yourself will deny you personal growth, professional or business opportunities, as well as life experiences.

So, here are tips to get you out of your cocoon. Don't forget to start with the hardest part.

> ### Take That First step

What you need to get started is that first step. It may not be easy at first. Nothing comes easy as well. The first day at work is boring, the same as going to the gym. But when you continually build your stamina, your motion will become easier. Take the first step to achieve your dream!

> ### Inspire Yourself

Don't wait for extrinsic motivation to make the first move. Discover your inner motivation! It could be a motivational video, TED Talks, Lifehack articles, riverside, or a walk in the park. Ensure it is something that drives you to take action. Inspiration is a motivational tool to help you push yourself.

> ### Create Your Environment

You need the right environment to succeed and make good choices. It is better to read at your desk than to read on your bed. If you want to stay healthier and fit, put healthier foods and water closer to you. Avoid junk and exercise your muscles daily. Also, avoid toxic relationships. Stay around people who will constantly remind you of your goals and aspirations.

➢ **Avoid the Safe Choice**

You can group your choices into two – the safer ones and the daring ones. Go for the ones that will enable you to dare the impossible and teach your invaluable lessons. You cannot grow by succumbing to safer choices. Get out of your comfort zone and explore new frontiers.

➢ **Visualize the Next Level**

What would it look like to be happily married, successful in your business and career, and touching lives? Visualize those dreams! Visualization will enable you to focus more on your goals and achieve success. It will help you know where you want to be and what you need to do to get there.

➢ **Learn From Other Victors**

Whatever level of success you want to achieve, someone has had it already. Learn from them and pick cues and lessons on how they overcame the barriers. Read their books, online journals, interviews, and podcasts.

➢ **Do What Scares You**

Ask yourself when you are taking on new projects: Does this task scares me? If yes, then do it! That's how you face your fear and win. See every difficult task as a frog, then eat the frog!

➢ **Work on Your Weaknesses**

There are self-imposed limits, and most of them are products of our weaknesses. It could be bad habits, poor self-esteem, or physical limitation. Weaknesses make a big mountain look unsurmountable, and they can limit you from achieving the success you desired. You can turn your weaknesses into strengths.

➢ **Seek for Help**

A little bit of assistance can be so significant in facing resistance. Having someone to support you can counterbalance the impact of any negative thought pattern that may limit you. It could be a life coach, mentor, spouse, friend, parent, or accountability partner. They can assist you to make the push you need to get out of your comfort zone.

Final Thoughts

You have to push yourself past limits to reach your goals. There is no alternative to greatness other than sacrificing your comfort zone and accomplishing great things.

Life does not reward complacency or mediocrity. But by pushing yourself, you can break through barriers and trek the paths that men have not trodden. And interestingly, once you break through the limits, you will be amazed why you never thought the challenges are surmountable. Accept your limits so you can grow beyond them!

How to Stay Motivated to Start a Business

What's your motivation for starting a business? Here's how to find and sustain your drive for business ownership.

Flexibility, control, and legacy are common entrepreneurial motivations.

Being in the right headspace helps you maintain your entrepreneurial motivation when challenges arise.

A positive attitude, meditation, and a strong support system can help you sustain your enthusiasm for running your business.

At the base of every business is the ardor and dedication of an entrepreneur with a goal. Working for yourself is an incredible feat that can be extremely challenging. Many resolutions rest on your shoulders, like the structure of your business, company culture, and even whether your company continues to run. It's a lot for one person to carry, and sometimes running a business feels overwhelming.

It's not always disorganization or a lack of cash flow that brings a company to its knees. Enthusiasm can be short-lived, and a negative attitude is a silent killer. As our emotions shift, it can be hard to keep that passion for your business steady, especially when new challenges come along. Fortunately, there are many ways to manage and sustain your motivation so you don't burn out.

Why is Motivation Important for an Entrepreneur?

Motivation is important for an entrepreneur for the same reason fuel is important for a plane: Nothing gets off the ground without it. A business isn't always booming with profit or celebrating achievements. Completing mundane or difficult tasks is a daily necessity, and it's your ambition that will push you through it to keep striving for your goals.

"Motivation can boost an entrepreneur's confidence to match their goals," Shagun Chauhan, a business consultant for iFour Technolab, told business.com. "Recognition, esteem, and self-actualization fulfill you. Motivated thoughts allow you to think more productively and experiment with new ideas."

Your drive is also tied to your dopamine reward pathways, which make you want to keep going or do something again, said Teralyn Sell, licensed psychotherapist, and owner of Inner Strength Counseling and Recovery. "Motivation is the workhorse behind your ideas."

How do I Sustain my Motivation when Starting a Business?

There are several ways entrepreneurs can sustain motivation when starting a business. Follow this expert advice to find the best tips that work for you.

✓ **Be in the Right Headspace.**

Being in the right headspace is important. To stay motivated, you can't allow fear of failure or bumps in the road to knock you off your path. When you focus on your strengths, the future of your company becomes clearer. Your general mindset is a crucial factor in sustaining your positive energy.

"Think of the Little Engine That Could," Sell said. "He knew he wanted to get over the mountain to bring the toys to all of the boys and girls on the other side. And when self-doubt began to creep in, the little engine repeated over and over to himself, 'I think I can, I think I can.' As new business owners, it's imperative you do the same."

Starting a business can be overwhelming, and it can be difficult to stay motivated when you hit a roadblock. When those issues arise, so does fear, which is why protecting your headspace is key to overcoming them.

✓ **Use Meditation to Reflect.**

Breaking down your process to understand exactly what is needed to complete your workload is recommended. He also recommends meditation to help you clear out your thoughts and focus on the progress you've made. This reflection strengthens your fortitude against stress or disappointment and pushes you to learn from your past mistakes.

Practice daily mindset shifts, Put out positive energy and create some new neurological pathways to keep you going. It's easy to slip down in the dumps when things get tough, but mental toughness is key to your success."

✓ Surround Yourself with Motivational People.

Aside from having a good attitude, it's important to surround yourself with like-minded people who share your goals. Not only will this give you a support system, but being around other motivated individuals who encourage you and hold you accountable makes it harder to quit. A good group of successful people can inspire you and keep you on the right path.

✓ Create a Strong Mission Statement.

Don't underestimate the importance of your mission statement either. A strong mission statement that you and your employees understand and believe in can help you set company goals, avoid missteps, and stay motivated when you face rough patches.

✓ Focus on your Mental Health.

If you find that your determination ebbs and flows, this fluctuation might be due to your mental health. When you have an imbalance of neurotransmitters like dopamine or serotonin, your enthusiasm is more apt to burn out.

"You might start off with a dopamine push like, 'What a great idea!'. "But [when you] lack drive or reward, you fizzle out. If you are stressed out, your cortisol might be impacted, and you may feel fatigued or depressed. If this sounds like you, then get those levels checked out before your big idea gets off the ground."

✓ Focus on your Physical Health.

Starting a business is a big venture that requires a lot of time and energy. Many aspiring entrepreneurs pay so much attention to their new business that they forget to focus on themselves. It may not seem important, but your physical health can play a major role in your motivation to keep going. Drinking a lot of water, eating balanced meals, and getting enough physical exercise will help keep your body running efficiently so you can focus on creating a successful business.

Additionally, one of the biggest mistakes a new entrepreneur can make is burning the candle at both ends. Getting enough sleep each night is imperative to maintaining long-term motivation. There is often no task so important that it can't be left until morning – and with a well-rested mind, it may be easier to accomplish the next day anyway.

✓ Plan Ahead.

Planning ahead and setting reminders can help you stay on track throughout the day. Create a schedule of the things you want to accomplish each day, week, month, etc. Set alarms each day to remind yourself when it's time to focus on specific tasks and when it's time to take breaks. There are productivity apps that can help with this as well.

✓ Set a Realistic Schedule for Yourself.

One way to achieve goals and stay motivated is by understanding your working habits and creating a realistic process that coincides with them. For example, if you are not a morning person, setting the goal of waking up at 4:30 am every day might result in you accidentally over-sleeping, derailing your daily schedule, and ultimately giving up. Instead, shift your working hours later in the day (or whatever schedule works best) to create a realistic workday that you are likely to adhere to.

✓ Incentivize Yourself.

Everyone loves a reward. When you're starting a business, it can be easy to get so focused on "what's next" that you forget to celebrate the little victories. Keep track of your milestones – big and small – and reward yourself when you reach them. Recognizing each challenge and achievement is a great way to remind yourself how far you've come and what you've accomplished.

✓ Create a Routine.

The best way to motivate yourself long-term is to create a routine. Studies say it takes the average person between 18 and 254 days to form a new habit, and 66 days for a new behavior to become automatic. Create a routine to stay on track – if you stick with it long enough, you may just be automatically motivated to work without having to think twice.

What are the types of Entrepreneur Motivations?

Contrary to popular belief, money isn't the only motivator. Entrepreneurial motivations include flexibility, control, and legacy, said Jacent Wamala, licensed therapist and owner of Wamala Wellness.

Each motivation falls under one of two categories – intrinsic or extrinsic motivation. Intrinsic motivation is the internal form of motivation that comes from a personal desire to fulfill your goals and achieve individual ambitions and personal satisfaction. Extrinsic motivation is driven by external rewards like money, praise, and fame.

Flexibility is a valuable benefit of entrepreneurship. Working for a company or someone else might require long hours that leave you feeling overworked, overextended, or bored. When you work for yourself, you may still put in long hours – maybe even more than you would be working for someone else – but you have the freedom to structure those hours how you want.

Control is similar to flexibility in terms of power over your own goals and productivity. More importantly, you have direct control over your success and livelihood. While calling the shots is freeing, it does require you to be reliable and efficient.

Legacy in business is the desire to create something long-lasting that can produce generational wealth, with value or an impact on a wide group of people that lasts lifetimes. A successful business can span multiple generations.

Understanding your motivation and what drives you will help you focus on your goals. When your underlying purpose is clear, you won't feel as overwhelmed or discouraged when things change or you encounter obstacles.

Having a solid understanding of why you are starting a business will remind you of the necessity to continue in the face of adversity.

What makes a Great Entrepreneur?

One of the characteristics of a successful entrepreneur is resilience. A good businessperson plan for obstacles, learns from failures, and chooses to keep moving forward.

"Write down your lessons and wins regularly," Wamala said. "Create boundaries to avoid burnout. Seek peer support or mentorship to have a community that you feel understands you. A great entrepreneur is flexible and a lifelong learner."

CHAPTER NINE

ENTREPRENEURSHIP AND YOUR MENTAL HEALTH

Entrepreneurship is inherently lonely.

When you embark on this journey, it's important to note just what you're getting into. I'm not just talking about the struggles and achievements that you're going to be embarking on, but the personal investment you're about to make.

In this particular instance, with your mental health.

You see, the reason I am writing this particular topic is because some of the most talented, successful, and driven entrepreneurs I have ever met are, most often, the most depressed.

They lack the feeling of fulfillment. They feel isolated. They're stuck in a mental corner, so to speak.

From an outsider's perspective, that might seem a bit crazy. How can someone who has created their own destiny, been accomplished and driven success, feel this way?

It's not as Unimaginable as you Might Think.

For most of you who become an entrepreneur, you quickly realize, you can't share this journey with most. Yes, you may have loved ones, friends, even a significant other to confide in about your struggles, successes, journey, but do they truly understand it from your perspective? After all, you're the one going through the grind.

For some, you have a founding team, a partner to work with, which can help release some of the pressure, but for most, it's truly just you.

Yes, you can have employees too, but for a long part of your internal battles, you don't want to share such things with them as you would with perhaps a founding team. You're the one on top. This is your battle to overcome.

On top of that, think about the mindset you need to have as an entrepreneur. You can't become complacent. You can't lose your hunger. You can't lose your drive to succeed.

Understanding that, think about how draining it can become if you never truly celebrate your accomplishments, or always take the next accomplishment as the minimum you now need in order to grow.

Now that we have painted a clearer picture, it is easy to see how many of the most successful entrepreneurs deep down can feel alone.

How Can you Overcome this?

How can you maintain feeling fulfilled, happy, and driven?

The biggest thing is about being self-aware and understanding all of these factors listed above (and much more that are personalized to each given situation).

We all battle these hurdles. It's part of understanding your DNA, your ego, your outside factors as to why you are doing what you are doing. When you understand better why you have such feelings and what stems from them, you can better understand how to deal with them.

Another thing that I have found many successful entrepreneurs do to overcome such mental fatigue — and yes, something that even I do myself — is seek professional help via therapists.

This isn't the 1950s anymore, the negative stigma to therapy shouldn't exist. In fact, it can become an asset to have someone from a professional perspective to hear your thoughts, feedback, emotions and give you recommendations and thoughts back.

We go to the gym to keep our bodies healthy and strong. We eat healthy to keep our minds sharp and our bodies going. Approach going to therapy to keep your mindsets aligned in the right direction for the long term and to remain 100% focused.

Above all, with everything stated above, focus your mental being on positivity. Look into things that are proven to allow you to focus on positive energy, positive results. Yes, they all take work and consistency. However, you're an entrepreneur. You already know how to work hard. No reason to make any excuses.

Why is this an Important Conversation to have and Bring up Here?

First, we as entrepreneurs, need to always be on our A-Game. We have clients and customers that depend on us, employees that depend on us, families that depend on us, and expenses we need to always be covering. This can drag you down and put you into an emotional rut if you let it. You need to be aware of this and leverage it as a strength, not a weakness.

Second, we need to be open about these personal obstacles because the struggles of growing a company aren't your only struggle. We have the struggle of being a human too. By being open about such things, we can better figure out solutions, talk to ourselves, work together to overcome these emotional ruts.

Your mental health is important. It's as important as your physical health, your diet, and the success of your company. None are mutually exclusive. Be self-aware about what makes you tick, what stresses you out, what puts you into a positive, fulfilled mindset. Spend time asking yourself the tough questions and exercising your brain. The more often you do, the more consistently that you do, the better, more successful, you will be.

12 Ways to Manage your Mental Health as an Entrepreneur

Did you know, over 70% of entrepreneurs experience poor mental health?

This can be anything from stress to burnout to breakdown - and we here at Calmer know that it's all preventable.

Whether you are planning on launching your business, working freelance, or have been running your own business for several years, it's important to prioritize your mental health and wellbeing.

Here are 12 tips on how to start supporting your mental health, as well as further support you can follow:

- **Take Note of any Negative Feelings**

Entrepreneurs are particularly likely to experience stress compared to the working population. Entrepreneurial stress is commonly caused by uncertainty, loneliness, and financial concerns, and it can escalate without the right support.

Tania Diggory, Founder of Calmer, wrote in Psychologies Magazine that entrepreneurs need to get comfortable with being uncomfortable. "Every day presents different challenges as an entrepreneur ... the entrepreneur lifestyle demands that you take calculated risks, try new things, find solutions and make bold moves ... this can feel highly overwhelming and have a profound impact on a person's mental health and wellbeing."

One particularly productive way of managing your negative thoughts and feelings is to accept them fully. Take note, let them wash over you, and give yourself time to address what is causing them.

- **Identify What is Contributing to your Stress**

This leads us to our next step: identifying what is contributing to your stress. Running a business - especially in the early stages - can be overwhelming, consuming all of your time and energy. With every entrepreneur, there will be recurring situations that cause a high amount of stress - that may be your workload, your business' financial uncertainty, or your fear of the unknown.

Identifying what makes you feel stressed is the first step in preventing that stress from happening again.

- **Disconnect your Business' Value and your Own Self-worth**

There's a tendency for entrepreneurs to define themselves by the success of their business ventures - this can be unhelpful, especially for our mental health.
In difficult cases, entrepreneurs can end up spending more time on their business, trying to make things work, and neglecting their friends, family, and life outside of work. Make time to practice self-love, and realize that the figures on the balance sheet don't define who you are, or what you're worth.

- **Define your Zone of Genius**

When you started working for yourself, you probably took up the roles of a whole team of people: you were the CEO, the Finance Director, and the Sales Manager, all at the same time. However, you probably don't want to carry on this way, and in fact, you'll find it unproductive to do so.

It's time to define your zone of genius. This is essentially the role and accompanying activities that you're great at, as well as those you enjoy.

Working in your zone of genius will equate to you finding more joy in your work, and getting better results too. For the roles that don't fit you, it's time to start delegating these…

- **Hire Outside Help**

  …by hiring outside help. Many small businesses are run on a shoestring budget, and that includes freelancing. However, sourcing people to help you manage your business is a good step to growing your business and increasing its chances of success.

  You (probably) wouldn't attempt to do your own company accounts, so you've hired an accountant. The same model can be used for zones outside of your own zone of genius.

  If you struggle with balancing the books, a bookkeeper on an hourly rate can help. Too many emails? Try a virtual assistant. Want to create a high-quality video series? Find a local videographer.

- **Build your Support Network**

  You've heard of a business network, but what about a support network? Alongside building a team to support you with business tasks, try building a support network of stakeholders who care about you and your business alike.

  These can be friends, family, suppliers, mentors, or customers - have a read of our guide to building your entrepreneurial ecosystem for more information.

- **Make the Most of your Working Hours**

  To achieve a good work-life balance, it's important to set yourself working and stick to them. While this may seem impossible in the beginning, hacks like putting your working hours in your signature will start preparing your clients for your downtime, and will in turn manage their expectations.

If you want to learn how to manage your time effectively, find your feet as an entrepreneur, and build your personal resilience.

- **View Downtime as an Investment in Productivity**

Alongside productive working hours, giving yourself ample downtime is crucial. In its most simple sense, getting a good amount of rest and sleep can improve your productivity at work. You will also be more motivated while at work, knowing you have free time to enjoy and work towards.

- **Be Your Best Boss**

Many entrepreneurs find themselves working far more than they would ask an employee to do for them. As a recap over points 7 and 8 - give yourself fair working hours, enjoy your downtime, and treat yourself how you would a team member.

What one step could you take today to transform the way you manage your time, and as a result, create a kinder approach to your working days?

- **Don't go Searching for Happiness**

Entrepreneurs are often portrayed as superheroes of the business world - they've broken the mold, reinvented the wheel, and thought outside the box!
Working for yourself can often feel like the opposite. And that expectation - of having it all together - can make it even harder to recognize your weaknesses and stop yourself from expecting big successes.

Instead of focusing on happiness highs, try focusing on contentment. Contentment is a mental or emotional state of satisfaction, often drawn from being comfortable in your mind, body, and surroundings. It can be achieved through practice, and over time we can start to feel more content in ourselves and our businesses.

- **Improve your Mental Resilience**

As well as shifting your focus from happiness to contentment, building up your mental resilience will enable you to weather the low periods of running a business.

A good business leader is one that can stay positive in the face of adversity, thinking clearly despite negative situations that may be out of your control. We all have the capacity to become this person, it just takes practice to get there.

Remember: Business is a Marathon, not a Sprint

Integrating many of these short-term practices we have listed will help you to manage your business in the long term. Be kind with yourself, and know that you're not alone.

CHAPTER TEN

HOW TO FIND YOUR CALLING AS AN ENTREPRENEUR

What path is best when establishing a business? There are, arguably, two paths that an entrepreneur can take. The first is to follow the needs of the market and build a business plan on solving the world's biggest problems and by doing so they think they will achieve success and change the world. The other path an entrepreneur can follow is to listen to their calling, their passion, and pursue it. Having tried both paths in my entrepreneurial past, I feel very strongly that the second path is the one that entrepreneurs should follow. As it turns out, following your passion and being a hero in business are not mutually exclusive.

Following The Market Alone Does Not Work

Let me tell you a story when my friend started his business, "Little You", He was following his passion. Originally part of a school project, He wanted to nurture children's creativity through building custom, 3D-printed avatars and felt it was a great way to solve the problem of creativity scores dropping drastically as children grow into adults. As a creative person himself, He felt passionate about this business and wanted nothing more than for it to succeed. However, as he did more research and dug further into the subject of creativity scores in adults, He learned that solving this problem would not change the world, and that little could be done to maintain creativity scores from age five to age 30. He also discovered that the market for custom avatars is part of a niche category, and not as large as he initially thought.

From there, He decided to follow the trend and adapt to what he thought the market wanted. He gave up on "Little You" and started a business called U-Dimensions. U-Dimensions would offer a free marketplace for video game companies to produce and sell 3D-printed merchandise and marketing materials. After four years of working on U-Dimensions, He realized he wasn't following his passion and was left feeling unfulfilled. He decided to follow his passion and resume working on "Little You". He resolved never to give up on my passion ever again.

When an entrepreneur does not feel passion for their business, it will not fulfill their motivational needs, and the business is doomed for failure in the long run – regardless of how successful the business is.

Experts Agree that Passion is Important for your Business

Many well-known entrepreneurs have spoken publicly about the importance of finding a calling or following your passion.

For example, Apple CEO Steve Jobs' commencement speech at Stanford University in 2005 has become known as the "follow your heart" speech. He recalls a quote that he heard at the age of 17, and the impact it had on him:

... 'If you live each day as if it was your last, someday you'll most certainly be right'... since then, for the past 33 years, I have looked in the mirror every morning and asked myself: 'If today were the last day of my life, would I want to do what I am about to do today?' and whenever the answer has been 'no' for too many days in a row, I know I need to change something... Remembering that you are going to die is the best way I know to avoid the trap of thinking you have something to lose. You are already naked. There is no reason not to follow your heart.

Arguably one of the most successful and brilliant entrepreneurs of our time had about fifteen minutes to tell these young people anything he wanted, and he chose to talk about doing something that you love and following your heart.

Another famous example is Phil Knight, the founder of Nike, in his 2016 memoir Shoe Dog writes:

I had an aching sense that our time is short, shorter than we ever know, short as a morning run, and I wanted (my life) to be meaningful. And purposeful. And creative. And important. Above all... different. ...I'd tell men and women in their mid-twenties not to settle for a job or a profession or even a career. Seek a calling. Even if you don't know what that means, seek it. If you're following your calling, the fatigue will be easier to bear, the disappointments will be fuel, the highs will be like nothing you've ever felt.

Knight goes through the early years of Nike making almost no money, but he was so passionate about his shoes that he persevered and eventually found success.

There are hundreds of other quotes that can be found like the above from people such as Richard Branson (founder, the Virgin Group), Oprah Winfrey (media mogul), David Karp (founder, Tumblr), and many, many more.

I realized that following my passion in business would result in the following:

- The business will have a vision based on what drives me.
- Passionate business owners sell more effectively because they care, and it shows.
- Having passion helps to build authenticity into the business plan and brand.
- It will bring clarity when feeling doubtful.
- Feeling motivation to develop and grow the business.
- Surrounding myself with like-minded individuals to network with.
- Setting my business apart from competitors.

It is not easy to start a business, and a new business is often built on sweat equity. Without passion, there cannot be enough motivation to stick with it and see it through its startup phase into the growth phase. If you do not have a passion for your business, it will be too easy to quit and move on to something else.

How can you Build a Business Based on your Passion?

Establishing what you are passionate about is the number one most important thing to building a business based on your passion. Finding the thing that you love to do can be challenging and might go through several phases of metamorphosis before you find a viable business opportunity that you can thread your calling into. Finding your calling as an entrepreneur is the adult version of "what do I want to be when I grow up?" and then making a plan that allows that business to thrive.

If your passion can't integrate into your business directly, don't forget it. I think that most people's passionate callings can be involved in their entrepreneurial business plans in some way. But if there is no way to build a business around your passion, you can still integrate it into your working life indirectly. For example, if you are an accountant, but your true passion is mountain biking, surround yourself with things that remind you of riding. Fill your office with photographs and memorabilia that bring you joy during your workday or network some of your client base from mountain biking groups.

Remember that passion is infectious to those around you. When you fuse your passion and your business, you are bound to find success. Not only will you never give up on your dreams, but your demeanor and love of your business will also shine through. Every presentation you have with investors, every sales interaction, every fulfilled order will leave your customer with a sense of second-hand passion. They are going to love your product because you love it so much.

Don't be afraid to follow your passion. Being afraid of failure is something that most entrepreneurs will face. It is a perfectly valid way to feel, and for some, everything is at risk. However, it is better to fail at doing something you love and to learn from those mistakes, than to be afraid of failing and never follow your calling. ("Success is walking from failure to failure with no loss of enthusiasm" – Winston Churchill)

I genuinely hope that my story and advice have resonated with you. It took me many years and a little bit of failure to find that following my passion was the right thing to do for me and my business. I will never forget the lessons learned from following what I thought was a good business plan and leaving behind the thing I cared about the most. I will continue to work towards growing my business with all the love and devotion that I can. I know that by doing this, I am not solving a huge world issue, but I am making myself happy and I know I will continue to find success. Remember, pursue your calling, and success and happiness will follow.

4 Key Ways How Entrepreneurs Take Business Opportunities

They say that opportunity only knocks once. In the business world, however, opportunities do not get the chance to knock before they are shoved through the door.

You see, entrepreneurs take business opportunities very seriously. Serious entrepreneurs do not wait for an opportunity to come to them. They study their environment and find the opportunity. Opportunity counts for so much in the business world. Whenever you encounter an opportunity, you need to grasp it and submit it to your will. Entrepreneurs treat business opportunities differently. Here are some views of entrepreneurs on how to take advantage of business opportunities:

#1 Seduction

With one wrong move, a business opportunity can fly out of your grasp. Thus, you need to study the opportunity. Is it mysterious? If so, what could it be hiding? What can help you pull that opportunity towards you?

Seduction of the business opportunity is a game of balance. You cannot be too eager or the opportunity will get suspicious and pull away. You cannot be too aloof, or the business opportunity will go to other entrepreneurs. You have to show that you are the proper person to get that opportunity. You have to treat it with the proper respect. After all, you are the entrepreneur who needs that opportunity.

#2 Prey

Some entrepreneurs think business opportunities are like prey. They enjoy the thrill of hunting for a perfect business opportunity and take them down for the kill. For these entrepreneurs, business opportunities should be watched out for.

These people watch their environment, hoping for any sign of business opportunities. Constant vigilance is their creed, and nothing can stand in the way of their success. By taking this mindset, you gain the instinct of the hunter. You become very competitive in terms of taking business opportunities. Sometimes, this is a good thing, leading you to your success.

There are times, however, when this mindset can lead to your downfall. Hunters often love the thrill of the hunt, but neglect to take care of the opportunity once they have them in their hands. You know that you need to take care of every opportunity in order for it to be of any use to you.

#3 Plant

Smart entrepreneurs view business opportunities as plants. They plant the seeds of opportunity and nourish it to make it grow into a successful business venture.

This view of business opportunities is probably the best considering the fact that opportunities really do need to be taken care of in order for an entrepreneur to achieve success. Getting the opportunity is just the start of being an entrepreneur. In order to gather the fruits of success, an entrepreneur should be able to not only get the opportunity but expand it.

#4 Luck

Some entrepreneurs see business opportunities as lucky coincidences or even a work of fate. They, of course, keep a lookout for business opportunities. However, they do not actively work to find some.

This entrepreneur's view of business opportunity is probably the most naïve in today's world. As was mentioned earlier, opportunities nowadays have very little chance of falling into someone's lap. By waiting for the business opportunity to come to you, you are probably wasting your time.

What you need to do is get up off that chair and start looking at your environment and make the opportunity for yourself. What are the advantages to this? Well, if you create your own opportunity, then you'll have direct access to it and have intimate knowledge of how to shape it into a great business venture.

Another plus to creating your own business opportunity is that you will be getting a head start. This means that you can forget about the competition taking your opportunity and beating yourself to the success that you so anticipated.

So how should entrepreneurs view business opportunities? Well, the best thing you can do is take all of the different views and try to balance them into your own view. Remember that different things work for different people. Try not to conform yourself to other entrepreneurs' views of business opportunities. This way, you can be at your most effective.